T0247892

A MYSTERY FROM THE MUMMY-PITS

A MYSTERY FROM THE MUMMY-PITS

The Amazing Journey of Ankh-Hap

Frank L. Holt

OXFORD
UNIVERSITY PRESS

OXFORD
UNIVERSITY PRESS

Oxford University Press is a department of the University of Oxford. It furthers
the University's objective of excellence in research, scholarship, and education
by publishing worldwide. Oxford is a registered trade mark of Oxford University
Press in the UK and certain other countries.

Published in the United States of America by Oxford University Press
198 Madison Avenue, New York, NY 10016, United States of America.

Library of Congress Cataloging-in-Publication Data
Names: Holt, Frank Lee, author.
Title: A mystery from the mummy-pits : the amazing journey
of Ankh-Hap / Frank L. Holt.
Other titles: Amazing journey of Ankh-Hap
Description: New York : Oxford University Press, [2024] |
Includes bibliographical references and index.
Identifiers: LCCN 2023033832 (print) | LCCN 2023033833 (ebook) |
ISBN 9780197694046 (hardback) | ISBN 9780197694053 (epub)
Subjects: LCSH: Mummies—Egypt. | Mummies—Texas.
Classification: LCC DT62.M7 H65 2024 (print) | LCC DT62.M7 (ebook) |
DDC 393/.3—dc23/eng/20230822
LC record available at https://lccn.loc.gov/2023033832
LC ebook record available at https://lccn.loc.gov/2023033833

DOI: 10.1093/oso/9780197694046.001.0001

Printed by Sheridan Books, Inc., United States of America

For Laura and Alec

CONTENTS

PREFACE

Mummified human remains remain human remains in spite of being mummified.

I have mumbled this mantra for most of my adult life. It reminds me that the act of mummification does not render a human being into the equivalent of a stone tool or a painted pot. An Egyptian mummy never ceases to be an Egyptian just because the body, or a portion thereof, appears in a sales catalog or lies in a museum display case.[1] To be, and ever to be—that is the quest of the mummified Egyptian. Their bodies were not preserved with our amusement or edification in mind, but as part of a complex set of beliefs to which they are still entitled. Only the deliberate dehumanization of mummies has made it possible in the recent past to turn them into food, paint, fertilizer, film props, or far worse—including celebratory fireworks explosions. People have found more ways to destroy millions of mummies than most of us would care to admit. Therefore, reader, beware: this book is about the treatment and mistreatment of dead people. In addition to discussions of decomposition, dissection, and dismemberment, readers must confront the unsettling consequences of cultural appropriation, colonialism, and commercial exploitation.[2] The guilty include us all, from professors and museum curators to comic book collectors and movie-goers.

The hope, however, is to make amends to at least one dead Egyptian whose remains have been horribly abused over the past several thousand years. By rediscovering and telling his story, we may perhaps restore some measure of his humanity. While well intentioned, can this be done without perpetuating a relentless cycle of ill treatment? Is the study of mummified remains itself an act of desecration? Should any mummy be on public display? Over a century ago, the famed anatomist Grafton Elliot Smith wrestled with many of these same issues when examining the royal mummies of Egypt. He wrote:

> One has to deal with subjects that may possibly give rise to offence, on the ground that it is not showing due respect to the memories of the powerful rulers of Ancient Egypt to display their naked remains, and use them as material for anthropological investigations. . . . Those who make such complaints seem to be unaware that the real desecration was committed twenty nine centuries ago by the subjects of these rulers; and that modern archaeologists, in doing what they have done, have been rescuing these mummies from the destructive vandalism of the modern descendants of these ancient grave-plunderers.[3]

Smith's remarks do not settle the matter squarely on the side of science. For example, the appalling treatment of Pharaoh Tutankhamun and his children by the anatomist Douglas Derry remains a travesty of scientific indifference.[4] Grafton Smith does, however, raise the important point that many mummies, whether royal or not, have needed rescuing. To find a mummy that someone has taken from its tomb and willfully damaged is a terrible thing, but to ignore the calamity is equally heartless. If that mummy can be saved from further destruction, properly housed, and respectfully studied by scientific and historical methods, then perhaps a service has been rendered to the past and present. The reader who persists through the following pages must judge whether any such benefit has been rendered to the mummy and memory of a man we now know to be named Ankh-Hap, the son of Maat-Djehuty.

The many years of interdisciplinary work described in this book could never have been accomplished by the author alone. I am deeply grateful to the many students, colleagues, and collaborators who have made this investigation possible. Their names can be found scattered in the text, notes, and Appendix 1; to any that I may have omitted as I look back over four decades of work, I offer a sincere apology.

It is my pleasure once again to thank Oxford University Press and its excellent editorial and production staff. I am especially grateful to executive editor Stefan Vranka for his learned advice and infectious enthusiasm for the written word. I thank also the press's anonymous peer reviewers. As always, my wonderful wife Linda has made my research and writing both possible and pleasurable. I treasure her wit and wise counsel every day. Last but never least, I dedicate this book to my daughter Laura and grandson Alec, who have kept me young in my lifelong pursuit of all things old, especially Egyptian mummies.

Chapter 1

The Mystery Begins

There simply must be a corpse . . . and the deader the corpse the better.

 —S. S. Van Dine, "Twenty Rules for Writing Detective Stories," 1928[1]

THE GUY ON THE GURNEY

On July 29, 1987, a borrowed hearse navigated the busy streets of Houston, Texas, with a mysterious body on board. The passenger had been dead for more than two thousand years, certainly long enough to satisfy S. S. Van Dine's seventh of twenty rules for a first-class detective story. My interest in this case fell under his rule number 6, which states that every detective story requires some sort of detective. In that role, I had arranged for the corpse to be transported across town by volunteers from a local funeral home. It was a short but significant trip, strange in its itinerary but stranger still in its outcome. The body was on its way from the Houston Museum of Natural Science to the Enhanced Oil Recovery Laboratory on the campus of the University of Houston (UH).[2] Seldom does an ancient corpse leave its coffin to visit a petroleum research facility, and rarer still does such a lab uncover things inside a human body that should never be there.

The person on the stretcher, draped in plastic, was an Egyptian mummy said to be named "Anh-Hr-H3cpj." The name sounded oddly futuristic, more suitable for a shipmate of the droids R2-D2 and C-3PO from the *Star Wars* saga than for someone from the distant past. Yet the deceased had borne that unusual alpha-numeric name since 1921 based on an early transcription of the prayer painted on the lid of the coffin from which he had come.[3] An updated reading would later transpose the name more correctly into "Ankh-Hap." As with other aspects of this mummy's puzzling his-tory, I could not at first be certain that the coffin and the name were both really his. Dead bodies have a habit of swapping places in the afterlife, as Egyptologists often discover when, say, a sarcophagus made for a deceased male is found to contain the remains of a female instead.[4] I had to consider whether the name "Anh-Hr-H3cpj" and its subsequent iteration "Ankh-Hap" reflected an early case of iden-tity theft by the passenger aboard the hearse. He posed for me the proverbial riddle wrapped in a mystery inside an enigma. The riddle would be the unexpected condition of his body; the mystery would be the oddly mismatched layers of his wrappings; and the enigma would be the smoke-stained coffin that had concealed them all.

ON THE CASE

The archaeologist and historian in the role of detective is a popular conceit in my academic profession, and I have plied it often.[5] Trained in the methodologies of historical study and mildly addicted to de-tective fiction, I have found it natural that ancient mysteries should be approached, solved, and explained as a Sherlock Holmes or Hercule Poirot might do. Both of these famous detectives have their Egyptological connections in literature, along with many others, such as the fictional sleuths Amelia Peabody and Philo Vance. The indomitable Peabody is the brainchild of an actual Egyptologist, Dr. Barbara Mertz, while Vance was conjured by writer S. S. Van Dine as an amateur investigator who reads hieroglyphics with ease and knows as much about ancient Egypt as any practicing Egyptologist. Vance even solves *The Scarab Murder Case* in which he must calm a gritty New York homicide sergeant, who whines: "Too many corpses. Why do these scientific bugs have to go digging up mummies and things? It's what you might call morbid."[6] In the case of Ankh-Hap, my detecting began quite unexpectedly on the morning of November 1, 1986. It was a Saturday, the day after Halloween, and I was visiting the Houston Museum of Natural Science (HMNS) with my wife and daughter. While there, we were surprised to see a mummy that we had never encountered on many previous excursions. The coffined corpse lay before us in the vast lobby like an island surrounded by a sea of puzzled faces. Rippling waves of patrons surged forward against the freestanding display case, paused, and then swept past to ogle other delights, but I held my place against the tide. I had a thousand questions about the person hiding in the shadows of the half-opened coffin, but most of them could not be answered. That was why, nine months later, the mummy was on board a hearse bound for my university.

In the interim, I had met with museum officials to suggest a research collaboration that might better investigate, explain, and exhibit the tattered mummy along with the coffin in which it rested. My efforts soon gave rise to the Houston Mummy Research Program (HMRP). As director of this joint venture, I began assembling a team of talented volunteers from both institutions. At first, we knew little about the mummy beyond its disheveled outward appearance and a few clues passed along to the museum from its former home at Texas A&M University in College Station. These materials included

Figure 1.1. The Mummy and Coffin of Ankh-Hap, early twentieth century

an old letter, a faded black-and-white photograph of the mummy propped up in its coffin (Figure 1.1), and two printed display labels giving a terse background history.[7] One of the labels declared:

AN EGYPTIAN MUMMY

THIS MUMMY WAS REMOVED FROM ITS TOMB IN EGYPT IN 1891 AND BROUGHT TO THE UNITED STATES. IT IS THE BODY

OF A PERSON OF SOME LOCAL IMPORTANCE, POSSIBLY A TAX
COLLECTOR OR OTHER REPRESENTATIVE OF THE RULER. . . .
THE CASE SUGGESTS THAT THE MUMMY DATES APPROXIMATELY
2000 B.C.

While this information seemed official and factual enough, I had some nagging doubts. After all, Sherlock Holmes had admonished, "There is nothing more deceptive than an obvious fact."[8] Confirming or refuting these "facts" about when the mummy was interred, what had been his status, and the date of his tomb's discovery called upon another of Holmes's maxims: "It is a capital mistake to theorize before one has data."[9] I needed more background information, but this was a classic cold case. The coffin and mummy had arrived on permanent loan at HMNS in 1970; both were officially registered many years later on June 26, 1985.[10] At that time, the condition of the anthropoid (human-shaped) wooden coffin was described as

poor; nose broken, beard missing. Paint badly abraded [sic] across front of head and hair. Many cracks and chips in painted surface. Wood appears dry and brittle.

The mummy itself was in worse shape:

Portions of body exposed, skull partially destroyed. Linen bindings loose, appears to have second cotton (?) binding at ankles, knees and around torso, securing arms to body and legs together. All wrappings at head removed exposing partially destroyed skull. Appears to have wood dowel running through neck into skull cavity. Assorted bones & wrapping debris along floor of coffin. Left toes missing.

These accession records listed the original collector as unknown. A note added: "Body has not been removed from coffin @ HMNS." That changed with the transport of the corpse to UH, but for what purpose?

Everyone had agreed that these invaluable artifacts deserved deeper historical documentation and closer scientific scrutiny. Therefore, HMRP resolved to investigate a series of key questions, unsure yet how far any of them could be answered. We began with these:

1. The riddle of the body: What was the condition of the mummy beneath its bandages? What pathologies were present? Was the body intact and, if so, why was a wooden dowel protruding from its neck? When had the front of the skull been so badly damaged?

2. The mystery of the wrappings: Were the cloth bandages of a uniform type and time? Were any decorative elements added to these wrappings? Were any objects such as amulets concealed among the layers?

3. The enigma of the coffin: What could the coffin tell us about the person for whom it was intended? Does the inscription painted on its lid suggest that the deceased was really a tax collector or similar official? Was the coffin originally constructed for this particular mummy, or were body and box mismatched at some point between ancient and modern times?

The first of these questions could only be answered by exploring beneath the wrappings that encased the mummy, but how should this be done? Two centuries earlier, mummies were often mutilated in the name of science. In 1792, the German anatomist Johann Friedrich Blumenbach toured England, borrowing mummies from various collections in order to saw them open for closer inspection.[11] He was interested in classifying racial types on the basis of skulls and faces, and also to ascertain which of the mummies available in Europe might be fakes corrupted by "artificial restorations and deceptions."[12] Examining a mummy often meant destroying it. Such ventures might partner scientific inquiry with showmanship before a gallery of wealthy ticketholders. In the early nineteenth century, "unrollings" of this type made household names of such men as John Davidson and Thomas Pettigrew.[13] On one occasion, the latter thanked a wealthy friend who purchased an Egyptian mummy and "with great kindness gave me liberty to do whatever I thought proper with it."[14] Immortalized in prose and poetry for his numerous demonstrations, he became known as "Mummy Pettigrew," while the press cleverly revised the Latin proverb *crescit amor nummi, quantum ipsa pecunia crescit* ("the love of money grows as the money itself grows") to read *crescit amor mummi, quantum ipse Pettigrew crescit* ("the love of mummies grows as Pettigrew himself grows").[15] Sometimes, with no pretense of scientific intent whatsoever, collectors staged "strip" parties in their own parlors for the delight of their dinner guests. When Pettigrew unrolled a mummy for a few friends in his home, a servant overheard him explain to his guests about hieroglyphics; she rushed to her compatriots in the kitchen and announced that the dead Egyptian was named "Harry Griffiths."

The days of parlor room dissections eventually passed, reminding us that what is acceptable, even lauded, in one era might become objectionable, even loathed, in another. HMRP of course had no intention of ripping into the bandages and body of Ankh-Hap. Answers about his life and death must come from external, noninvasive analysis. Fortunately, numerous advancements in medical science made this possible. A first step in that direction had been taken just a year after Wilhelm Roentgen's discovery of X-rays in 1895.[16] This procedure eventually became widespread for anatomical studies as well as for the detection of fake mummies and hidden amulets. In many early circumstances, however, the use of radiography was impractical, particularly during large archaeological rescue missions in the field. The activities of the Australian anatomist Grafton Elliot Smith offer an instructive example. In 1903, the mummy of Pharaoh Thutmose IV was unrolled before invited guests in Cairo's Egyptian Museum and later carried by horse-drawn cab to a nursing home to be X-rayed using the only radiograph machine in Egypt.[17] This work was undertaken by Elliot Smith and archaeologist Howard Carter, later to become the famous discoverer of King Tut's tomb. Smith examined dozens of mummies in Cairo, but his next assignment took him far from adequate medical facilities. Beginning in 1907, he accepted responsibility for the mummies being excavated in salvage operations ahead of flooding caused by the Aswan Low Dam. Elliot Smith is reported to have hastily unwrapped and dissected thirty thousand mummies during this period.[18] Not until the 1960s did portable machines make it practical to conduct more systematic and scientific X-ray examinations, for example to study the royal mummies in the Cairo collection or King Tut in his tomb.[19]

In a similar way, the invention of computer tomography (CT) marked a major step forward in medical imaging during the 1970s.[20] Unlike conventional X-rays, CT scans can capture discreet "slices" or cross sections of targeted areas within a human body, including soft tissues. This technology provides high-resolution images that may be viewed three-dimensionally rather than just two-dimensionally. The advantages of this procedure were as obvious to those examining Egyptian mummies in the 1970s as X-rays had been to their forebears in the 1890s.[21] Yet, as with early X-rays, the CT scanning of mummies proved too expensive and cumbersome to spread rapidly.[22] Most early CT projects required the serendipitous availability of a nearby hospital scanner during rare moments when the equipment was not booked to help living patients. Thus, many universities and museums did not begin CT scanning their mummies until decades later in the twenty-first century.[23] The newer radiological era of magnetic resonance imaging (MRI) has been less helpful. Mummified tissue, unlike living tissue, has been deliberately dehydrated, and this generally precludes the use of MRI scans because they rely upon a high moisture content.[24] Alive, we are essentially large sacks of water, but if properly mummified we are drained of liquids and become dry as toast. A mummified person loses up to 80% of his or her body weight. This renders the mummy almost invisible to conventional MRI, while CT scanners manage to explore desiccated corpses quite well. The problem is securing access to the expensive CT equipment.

For these reasons, the possibility of CT scanning the HMNS mummy seemed very remote in 1987. Then a stroke of luck opened an unexpected pathway to success. After lecturing about mummy studies in one of my undergraduate history courses, a student approached me after class with encouraging news: Did I know that there was a CT scanner on campus? It so happened that this student, Gautham Sastri, was assisting several UH scientists in their campus labs, one of which was equipped with a Deltascan 2000 fourth-generation CT scanner. This machine, donated by the oil industry, was being used in the Enhanced Oil Recovery Laboratory to examine core samples of the earth. Collaboratively, the UH Cullen Image Processing Laboratory was developing new software to process the data from these scans, relying in part upon a VAX/VMS-II/780 supercomputer provided by the UH Allied Geophysical Laboratory. Since these labs were constantly running test scans on random available objects such as cinder blocks to refine their software and display systems, why not use a mummy as one of the test subjects? It was a win/win situation for everyone at UH and HMNS.

In June 1987, I convened meetings of the principal scientists, curators, and staff of the HMRP to make final arrangements for the CT scan. Representatives from each of the labs participated, along with museum anthropologist Elisa Phelps as our museum program manager and student Gautham Sastri as our university program manager. The plan was ambitious. Without the usual time constraints imposed upon researchers by busy hospital schedules, we would be able to scan the mummy for days rather than just minutes. We were about to make Ankh-Hap the most thoroughly scanned human in history.[25] All was set, and a month later the HMNS mummy arrived at UH in its borrowed hearse—but I was not there to greet it.

STICKS AND BONES

Instead, I was at the University of Washington in Seattle, attending a National Endowment for the Humanities archaeology seminar on the Aegean Bronze Age. I fielded phone calls from the UH labs between sessions, gratified that everything was proceeding according to plan. The scan was a great success and generated immediate public interest. Local and regional news organizations sent photographers and reporters to cover what was happening to Ankh-Hap at UH. One newspaper headline read: "Tax man heartless? CAT scan may find out."[26] The story became more intriguing when the first images revealed not just the unexpected length of the wooden pole protruding at the neck, but a baffling array of other wooden rods inserted deep within the body (Figure 1.2).[27] The mummy appeared in worse shape than anyone had imagined. It consisted of real body

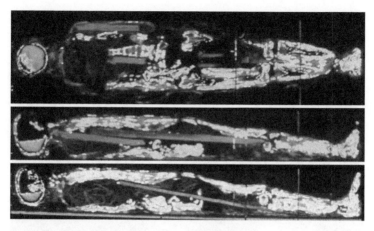

Figure 1.2. CT scans of Ankh-Hap, top and side views

parts alongside some fake ones. Ankh-Hap's back was broken, and much of his upper skeletal structure was missing. Oddly shaped masses were detected within his cranium. The mystery of the mummy intensified with every new pixel of data delivered from the cramped confines of the UH Enhanced Oil Recovery Laboratory.

The gleaming white machine produced hundreds of digital "slices" of the HMNS mummy spaced at intervals of five millimeters. These images were taken along the body's three axes: 403 segments from head to toe (Figure 1.3), 100 from side to side, and 60 from chest to back (Figure 1.4). This yielded a three-dimensional cube of data stored on four large reels of Epoch 480 magnetic tape with a density of 6,250 bpi (bits per inch).[28] Gautham Sastri processed these raw data by experimenting with the tools under development at UH for imaging geophysical samples. He refined the displays of pixelated data to create an early "fly-through" of the body, in this case more like a helicopter than airplane since the viewer may halt, hover, back up, or drop straight down and land anywhere along the journey. Despite the obvious damage to the head and a few missing

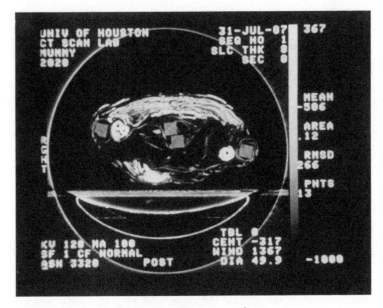

Figure 1.3. CT scan of Ankh-Hap, cross-section of torso

toes, the mummy gave the outward appearance of a complete body; however, the scan peeled away the layers of painted cartonnage (resembling modern papier-mâché) and linen wrappings to reveal the human wreckage underneath. The legs were intact, but the left part of the pelvis was damaged. Pieces of the right hand were visible where the left hand should be, and parts of the left hand had been relocated to the region of the left foot. Fake hands made from bundles of cloth were placed beside the fragments of real ones. The arms presented a puzzle of mismatched parts, with half the bones missing or incomplete. The spinal column was severed, with almost no skeletal structure above the lower thoracic vertebrae. Two cloth bundles found loose in the coffin were also scanned. One contained a pair of right ribs wrapped together, and the other held two additional right ribs with a part of the left scapula (shoulder blade).

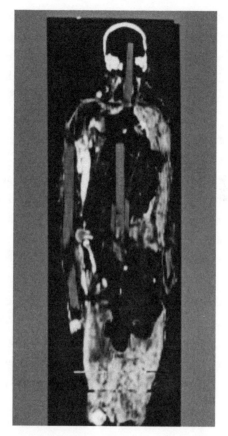

Figure 1.4. CT scan of Ankh-Hap, showing the network of wooden poles

This jumble made no anatomical sense. Major parts of the body were mysteriously missing or clumsily moved, but even more disturbing were the intrusive objects that should not have been inside the mummy at all: wasp nests in the skull and wooden sticks running through the corpse.

I knew that the condition of the HMNS mummy, strange as it appeared, was in some ways similar to others from Egypt. Some of these cases had resulted from ancient malpractice, particularly during the late first millennium BCE.[29] The pioneering Egyptologist Sir William Flinders Petrie recorded in his diary the recovery of many mummies, including the startling example of what was meant to be a small child:

> On pulling away the dummy sandals I found—not infantile toes, but a man's knee joint. I then pulled it to pieces, & found that the undertaker had not troubled to mummify the little brat at all; but had picked up, three old leg bones, & an old skull full of mud, & with scraps of old wraps on it; & the rascal had done them up tidily to satisfy the parental feelings, & put on a little gilt head-piece and sandals to look proper.[30]

Cases exist also of mummies braced by sticks and/or supplied with fake body parts by the ancient priests. In 1865, a mummy unwrapped in Quebec by James Douglas, son of the surgeon who also unwittingly brought the body of Pharaoh Ramses I to Canada, showed some physical anomalies.[31] The deceased was a young male:

> So crooked was he, that his embalmers—for the purpose of straightening him—passed a stick through the pelvis, transfixing the body. But that means failing, they bound him down to a heavy piece of wood, which they concealed among the bandages. The vertebral column is very much distorted, and the sternum lies almost upon the back bone.[32]

I learned that several Egyptian mummies with wooden rods inside them had been found in the British Museum collection. These included a priestess, an unidentified man, and an adult male whose detached head was secured to his body by a wooden stick.[33] Another example found in Chicago's Field Museum revealed an adult female with a wooden board running from her neck to pelvis.[34] The Rijksmuseum van Oudheden in Leiden housed a child's mummy that is missing the entire spine, pelvis, scapula, hands, and most of the ribs; fake hands were attached.[35] Other examples include a mummified woman whose right foot and both hands were placed inside her body, all three replaced anatomically with dummies; a woman with fake feet made of linen and reeds embalmed with her real toes and one kneecap tucked inside her torso; and the mummy of an elderly man having a linen dummy replacing his right hand.[36] Reminding us of Petrie's discovery, the body of another small boy was mutilated by embalmers in order to make him fit inside his tiny coffin.[37] This seven-year-old suffered the loss of both arms, and portions of his legs were cut away and discarded. More famously, a royal teenager named Tutankhamun lies incomplete in his coffin today, missing his rib cage and other body parts, whether from the trauma that killed him or from modern mishandling.[38]

Reunited with my team in Houston, we pored over the CT images and pondered all possible explanations. We wondered if Ankh-Hap had been the hastily buried victim of some horrible accident. Perhaps a crocodile or jackal had eaten the missing parts of him before his corpse could be salvaged, mummified, and wrapped. Or perhaps his grave had been robbed in antiquity, his mummy violated by treasure hunters, leaving it for later morticians to repair the damage as best they could. Was it possible that his condition had resulted entirely from modern mistreatment somewhere between Egypt and America? His body became a crime scene investigation.

We relied heavily on my colleague Dr. Rebecca Storey, a physical anthropologist at UH, to help make sense of the visible evidence. From the CT scans she produced a detailed osteological inventory of the incomplete remains. We followed this up with a direct examination of the exposed portions of the mummy, particularly the battered skull and some detached bones lying loose in the coffin, such as a cervical vertebra and a fragment of the maxilla (upper jaw). No part of the mummy was unwrapped or damaged as we crept carefully around the corpse, mindful that these were mortal remains and not a typical museum artifact made of stone or metal. I recall the musty, aromatic smell emanating from the mummy as a timeless tribute to the work of the embalmers.

Dr. Storey was able to fit together some of the loose bone fragments of the skull, demonstrating that it must have been fractured in relatively recent times, with several pieces scattered about the coffin. A fragment of the maxilla held a broken left molar and premolar, along with a broken root later identified for us by a volunteer dental surgeon, Dr. Corletta C. Trejo. These postmortem damages must have been inflicted with great force.[39] Compared to the old photograph that accompanied the mummy to HMNS, the head was now much more shattered. The picture shows a jagged hole in the forehead, but at that time the lower jaw was still intact. It would be important to establish when this modern vandalism occurred. Unfortunately, these damages made it impossible to attempt a reconstruction of the mummy's facial appearance, as is often done today.[40]

Despite these challenges, Professor Storey was able to compile an intriguing picture of the person inside the coffin. The deceased was confirmed to be a mature male. Sexing was based upon measurements of the mastoid, cortical thickness of the femur and tibia, and the subpubic angle. The ability to sex a mummified corpse using DNA analysis was thirty years in the future, when the FBI would assist in the study of Djehutynakht, an Egyptian nomarch (see the Glossary for this and other terms) excavated in 1915 and whose severed head now lies in the Museum of Fine Arts, Boston.[41] This forensic research would have delighted Djehutynakht's discoverer, Egyptologist George Reisner, another devoted fan of detective fiction whose personal collection of nearly two thousand murder mysteries was willed to Harvard's Widener Library.[42]

Ankh-Hap stood about five feet, four inches tall, based upon the length of his femur. He was therefore a bit short for Egyptian men at the time. He had died between the ages of thirty-one and fifty-one, most likely in his late thirties or early forties, as indicated by some of his cranial sutures. None of the bones showed signs of deformity, lifetime trauma, or healing. As a small child, however, the deceased had survived a bout of anemia associated with some physiological stress, perhaps a disease or malnutrition. He had begun to experience arthritic degeneration in his neck but not elsewhere in his body, which may favor an age in the late thirties rather than older. There were no obvious osteological signs of a composite "Frankenmummy" having, say, the bones of different individuals wrapped together on a wooden framework.

Ever since the discovery of calcified *Schistosoma haematobium* eggs inside two Egyptian mummies by the pioneering microbiologist Sir Marc Armand Ruffer in 1910, scientists have been examining mummies for evidence of ancient parasites.[43] We therefore invited specialists to review the scans, but they found no traces of the kinds of insects that sometimes afflicted an Egyptian's body or later invaded his or her corpse during or after mummification. Unfortunately, we had already found evidence of a modern infestation inside Ankh-Hap's head. Mud wasps, sometimes called dirt daubers, had at some point invaded the empty and exposed cranium. Two clusters of their multichambered nests show up in the images, each one empty; the hatchlings had all safely matured and

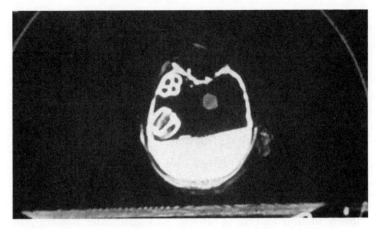

Figure 1.5. CT scan of Ankh-Hap, showing cranium with wasp nests

flown away years earlier (Figure 1.5). I would later correspond about these nests with Dr. Mark Greco, senior lecturer in Medical Imaging at Charles Sturt University in New South Wales, Australia. He is a pioneer in the use of CT-scanning technology in the field of entomology.[44] He pointed out to me that, while the earliest deliberate attempt to CT-scan bees' nests occurred in 2003, the HMRP had accidentally been first in 1987 when we captured images of these adobe-like structures. Ironically, these wasps have the scientific name *Hymenoptera* that sounds vaguely like the fictional Egyptian city Hamunaptra, the place of the dead in some mummy movies. Stranger still, these insects practice a form of mummification. Pregnant females capture small spiders and caterpillars, immobilize them with a sting, then wrap and seal them inside the nesting chambers to feed their hungry larvae. The wasps had gained access to the mummy's invitingly dry and shaded braincase through Ankh-Hap's fractured face. When and how this occurred, I would later discover.

DATING A MUMMY

We were making good progress on the first of our questions, but Ankh-Hap was no simple mummy. We chose to remove and test no samples from the human remains, so we stepped back and looked at the entire assemblage for further clues. Treating the coffin and its contents as a time capsule, we wondered if everything was buried together at the same time.[45] As mentioned earlier, it cannot always be assumed that an Egyptian coffin contains its original inhabitant.[46] Coffins could be reused in antiquity or randomly mated with an available mummy for sale in modern times. The unfortunate mathematics of Egyptian mummies is that coffins in museum collections generally outnumber bodies, the latter having been decreased by the ravages of nature and the negligence of collectors. An example may be found in an account by the nineteenth-century Greek antiquarian Giovanni d'Athanasi:

> An English traveller, had just bought the . . . mummy of the governor of Thebes, but having taken it into his head, whilst on his road to Cairo, that there might be some gold coins in this mummy, he caused it to be opened, and not finding any thing in it of the nature he sought, he threw it into the Nile, and gave the case belonging to it to Mr. [Henry] Salt.[47]

That coffin would eventually lie empty in the British Museum, while poor Soter—its lost human cargo—lay rotting in the waters of the Nile.[48]

I considered whether radiocarbon dating might help us to resolve the mystery confronting us: Do the textiles with the HMNS mummy really belong with the HMNS coffin? Were the wooden sticks already inside the body when it was buried, or were they added later? Were the wrappings and fake appendages part of the original interment? The radiocarbon method uses measurements of the radioactive isotope carbon 14 found in a sample of organic material to provide an estimate of when the source organism had died. Its use in Egyptology at the time was still relatively new and controversial; some scholars feared that the mummification processes themselves might distort the data. It had been recently argued, for example, that without further testing, carbon 14 dating "has little future in Egyptology."[49] We hoped that our HMRP investigation might contribute to that testing, and indeed radiocarbon dating has now become common in the study of mummies and related mortuary materials.[50]

The costs of carbon dating archaeological samples can be prohibitive, especially since the HMRP operated without dedicated funds of any kind. We relied solely on the generosity of interested partners and participants. In the spring of 1988, I appealed directly to the Radiocarbon Laboratory of the Balcones Research Center at the University of Texas in Austin. This facility agreed to help us free of charge by analyzing three samples offered by the museum: a tiny piece of wood from the coffin, a small segment of the loose cloth wrappings, and a sliver of wood from the exposed dowel that held the head in place. Each of these organic materials could be reached and removed without disturbing any part of the mummy.

The results from the radiocarbon lab were as surprising as anything we had seen so far. We suddenly had multiple time capsules, one inside the other. The coffin wood was determined to be 3000 ± 80 years BP (before the present, conventionally 1950). The cloth proved to be considerably younger, at 1630 ± 130 years BP. The wooden dowel was only 250 ± 70 years BP. At the time, these results were calibrated to mean that the coffin sample dated to 1130–970 cal

BCE with 68% probability (1 sigma, or one standard deviation) and 1210–890 cal BCE with 95% probability (2 sigma, or two standard deviations).[51] The cloth ranged from 190 to 450 cal CE with 68% probability, and 60–580 cal CE with 95% probability. The wooden dowel came from a tree felled between 1630 and 1770 cal CE with 68% probability, and from 1560 to 1840 cal CE with 95% probability.

As radiocarbon calibrations have improved over the years based on dendrochronology and other comparative research, it has been possible to revise these estimates. Today, with the assistance of Dr. Paula J. Reimer, an expert in the field of radiometric dating, we may refine these results using the CALIB REV8.2 Program and the IntCal20 calibration curve (Table 1.1).[52]

Without fixating on the calibrated date ranges per se, our main goal has been to discover the extent to which these materials might derive from the same historical period. Obviously, they do not. This chronological disparity deepened the mystery.

Early on, we consulted with Egyptologist Dr. Rosalie David about her experiences with Manchester Museum mummy 1770.[53] Unwrapped in 1975, the body of this ancient teenager had several curious features. Embalmers had treated the corpse as both male and female, supplying it with an artificial phallus as well as gold nipple covers. The left leg had been amputated below the knee and the right above the knee. Attached to the stump of the latter stretched a fake lower leg fashioned out of wooden splints, mud, and bandages. Reeds were used to simulate the toes. Clearly, the priests had been tasked with wrapping a body in such bad shape that they could not determine its gender and could only repair some of its worst damages. Radiocarbon dating showed that the body was at least a thousand years older than its wrappings. This suggested that a badly damaged mummy had been repaired and rewrapped in ancient times.[54] The similarities to Ankh-Hap were as fascinating to Dr.

Table 1.1 DATING THE PARTS OF THE MUMMY AND COFFIN

Sample	Radiocarbon Date	2 Sigma Calibration (relative probability)
Coffin wood	3000 ± 80 BP	1420–1010 cal BCE (100%)
Textile	1630 ± 130 BP	130–140 cal CE (0.5%)
		160–190 cal CE (1.8%)
		200–650 cal CE (97.7%)
Wood dowel	250 ± 70 BP	1470–1700 cal CE (60.3%)
		1720–1810 cal CE (25.3%)
		1830–1890 cal CE (5.7%)
		1910–1950 cal CE (8.7%)

David as they were for us. There was, however, the different problem of the modern-era dowel inside the HMNS mummy, which seemed from the CT scans to be consistent with the additional wooden braces otherwise invisible inside the body. UH biologists determined that the exposed dowel was coniferous in origin, cut from a pine, spruce, larch, or Douglas fir. This pointed to a likely source somewhere in North America.

Relative chronology placed the coffin wood very much earlier than the mummy's (re)wrappings, and the bracing stick very much later in modern times. In the CT scans, the two larger squared braces overlapped each other, one extending from the head to the lower chest and a longer one from the upper chest to the knees. Two more slender square poles, about half as wide, ran parallel down the body from the juncture of the larger braces down to the ankles. These four pieces were skillfully aligned, providing an integrated armature for the mummy. Unlike the fake arms and hands, this was clearly meant to provide a frame for the body rather than to replace a missing limb.

Egyptologist Charles Van Siclen III of San Antonio examined the coffin for more clues.[55] The six foot, three inch coffin is so thickly walled that the body barely fits inside it. The coffin has been plastered and painted, with an upper and lower half connected by eight mortise-and-tenon joints with locking wooden pegs. The lid features a carved human face, idealized rather than a true portrait, that is framed by a painted black wig that drapes behind the prominent ears and down the chest (Figure 1.6). The raised portions of the hair have been rubbed of paint by something pressing upon them, and the matching black beard has at some point been broken off and presumably stolen as a souvenir. There is also damage to the tip of the nose. A broad floral collar with sweeping bands of color and intricate design ornaments the upper body. On each side of this painted collar, the head of a falcon wearing a sun disk represents the god Horus (see the Glossary and Chapter 2). Figures of Isis and Nephthys also appear. These goddesses caress a totem of their brother Osiris. Below them on each side, Anubis makes an offering. Beneath the collar, the sky-goddess Nut spreads her protective wings across the body. Her hands hold aloft two feathers of the goddess Maat. Below, a coffin inscription has been painted in five columns. The text is framed by panels depicting the four sons of Horus, guardians of the internal organs removed from the body by the embalmers: Imsety for the liver; Qubehsenuef for the intestines; Hapi for the lungs; and Duamutef for the stomach. Beneath them kneel more figures of Isis and Nephthys.

Figure 1.6. Anthropoid wooden coffin of Ankh-Hap, showing damages

At the foot of the coffin, two facing jackals lie in their shrines. Along both sides of the lid, lined up behind twin images of the watchful lion-god Aker, eleven seated protectors wield knives to guard the mummy. On the base, a large *shen* ring signifies eternity and regeneration. The shallower bottom half of the coffin displays along its flanks a slithering white serpent. Placed directly on the mummy itself were additional decorations in the form of cartonnage panels. These have partially broken apart, but they depict another painted floral collar, another image of Nut with outstretched wings, and an "apron" covering the lower legs.[56] Van Siclen suggested that the coffin and cartonnage may have been the work of a single painter.[57] If so, this would make the present occupant of the coffin the likely person for whom it was intended. In other words, the mummy may actually be that of Ankh-Hap himself.

Dr. Van Siclen also retranslated the inscription painted across the lid of the coffin, updating the antique moniker "Anh-Hr-H3cpj" to Ankh-Hap (Figure 1.7). The prayer reads:

Figure 1.7. Anthropoid wooden coffin of Ankh-Hap, showing inscription

An offering which the king gives to Osiris, foremost of the Westerners, the great god, lord of Abydos,[58] to Ptah-Sokar-Osiris, the great god, lord of Shetayet,[59] to Anubis, lord of the necropolis, to Anubis, foremost on his shrine, to Atum, lord of Heliopolis, to Isis the great, the divine mother dwelling in . . ., and to Nephthys, the divine sister, that they might give invocation offerings of bread and beer, flesh and fowl, wine, milk, incense, oil, alabaster, fine linen, and everything good and pure, sweet and pleasant to the Ka of the Osiris[60] [named] Ankh-Hap, son of Padi (?), born of the lady Maat-Djehuty, justified, living forever and ever.

Van Siclen surmised that Ankh-Hap was buried ca. 350–250 BCE in a coffin made from extremely old, recycled wood. He believed the body of Ankh-Hap was vandalized by grave robbers and later rewrapped, but that this "could have happened 2000 or 200 years ago."[61] Closer inspection by an expert conservator confirmed that the coffin had at some point sustained extensive water and smoke damage, perhaps from exposure to a nearby fire.[62] I also consulted with Dr. Jonathan Elias, director of the Akhmim Mummy Studies Consortium. It is possible, in fact, that Ankh-Hap had been interred at Akhmim, an important religious site from which many mummies were ransacked between 1884 and 1888.

TELLING THE STORY

Our HMRP had uncovered a great deal of information since my first introduction to Ankh-Hap at the museum. We now had a better understanding of his name, age, and general health; his body's ravaged condition underneath the wrappings; and the range of dates between those wrappings and the wooden poles they concealed as well as the much older materials from which the coffin was made. I filed interim reports and published our preliminary findings.[63] Meanwhile, the museum organized an exhibition around the work of the HMRP entitled *The Egyptian Mummy: Unwrapping the Mystery*.[64] The story was told in three parts: the historical evolution of the mummification process, myths about mummies, and finally the application of modern technologies for the study of mummies such as Ankh-Hap. The exhibition featured large, illuminated panels from the CT scan as well as a video showing the scanning process.

The public and press responded enthusiastically.[65] There was, however, one complaint from a disgruntled taxpayer. He wrote to a local newspaper that research dollars should not be spent studying mummies, but rather on more worthwhile activities such as solving problems in the business world.[66] This objection missed the key point that we had spent no money at all, relying instead on volunteered equipment and expertise to achieve a worthy goal. In fact, the HMRP provided a model for what is today called crowdsourcing, a highly touted business strategy for obtaining needed services, ideas, or content by soliciting contributions from a large group of people.

None of this had been possible without an incredibly talented and generous team.[67] We had effectively served multiple campus and community interests through our combined efforts. In 1987, the HMRP was years ahead of its time as both a crowdsourced public history program and a digital humanities project. We managed not only to bring an ancient mummy into the age of nondestructive scientific analysis, but also to transport modern people back into the era when Ankh-Hap had lived and died. That is where we are headed next, before resuming our search along the pathways that brought him to America.

Chapter 2

A Life and Death in Egypt

The researchers—and now the public—know more about the mummy than they thought possible.

—Newspaper account, 1989[1]

WHO WAS ANKH-HAP?

With rare exceptions, ancient history tells the stories of pharaohs, queens, and conquerors, not of the common people. Most of the humbler masses left no trace of their brief existences in the shadowy wings of our vast world stage. Thus, for every Ramses, Cleopatra, or Alexander, there were millions of contemporary men and women now lost and sadly forgotten. Ankh-Hap was one of them, until the Houston Mummy Research Program shone some light into the darkness. He was no high-ranking tax collector from 2000 BCE, as once claimed on a museum placard, since his coffin lists no status or occupation of any kind and its design suggests a date some seventeen hundred years later. He was certainly no lofty kinsman of Pharaoh Tutankhamun nor a friend of Ramses the Great, as some journalists have speculated.[2] Yet he remains a man of flesh if not of blood, and his body and coffin demand of us some consideration of the humble life he once led. This requires a measure of speculation, of course, for as Hercule Poirot once explained: "You see, unless you are good at guessing, it is not much use being a detective."[3] So, based upon the times of his life as we know them from other sources, we may attempt a sketch of Ankh-Hap's experiences. This takes us back to a pivotal moment in history when Egypt teetered between the rival forces of native rulers and foreign invaders in the last decades of the fourth century BCE.

CHILD OF THE NILE

Under the divine protection of numerous deities, especially Bes and Hathor, a woman named Maat-Djehuty gave birth to a baby boy along the banks of the fertile Nile.[4] In another time and place, parents of a different religion might have named the child Abdullah ("Servant of God") or Theodore ("Gift of God"), but his ancient Egyptian father and mother chose Ankh-Hap ("The Apis Bull Lives").[5] This theophoric name honored a special deity, a sacred bull pampered at Memphis not far from the pyramids.[6] Since the beginning of Egyptian civilization, there had lived in succession one Apis bull at a time, each one a temporary vessel for the creator god Ptah's immortal spirit.[7] Symbolizing strength and courage, an Apis bull was selected based upon a prescribed pattern of twenty-nine markings, including white designs on an otherwise black body.[8] He was festooned and paraded about on holidays, fed the finest grains, and enjoyed his own harem of cows. Worshipers could walk up to a window and behold the exalted beast in his temple enclosure; they could anticipate cures and other divine favors while in his presence.[9] When he died, mourners mummified and buried him among all

Figure 2.1. Mummified Apis bull
Source: Andrea Izzotti / Shutterstock.com.

his forebears in a hallowed cemetery called the Serapeum (Figure 2.1).[10] This cult represented one of the oldest and most venerated in Egypt's long polytheistic history.

Egyptians craved this profound sense of continuity, of permanence rooted in repetition and sacred traditions. In a near-perfect world, why wish for change? Like the Apis bulls themselves, the past, present, and future should all look the same—hundreds of bulls and thousands of years with never a discernible difference from one to the next. As if by divine decree, everything in Egypt was ordered and immutable. Geography, religion, society, and government wove together seamlessly. The eternal Nile made Egypt possible.[11] It carved a narrow, fertile valley across the African desert, feeding its people and floating their wares from one town to the next (Figure 2.2). Like a long line drawn in the sand, the Nile bisected the inhabited earth, the sun rising on one side and setting on the

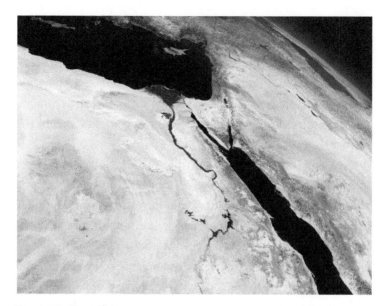

Figure 2.2. Egypt from space
Source: Harvepino / Shutterstock.com.

other in an endless procession of births, deaths, and rebirths. To be born in Egypt made it imperative to be buried there, for nowhere else on earth was quite like it. That is why the Egyptians, unlike their neighbors in Greece or Phoenicia, were reluctant to live abroad or to colonize across the seas.

In this self-obsessed land of a thousand gods, there lived the new mother, Maat-Djehuty, and her husband, Padi.[12] They were probably monogamous, wedded more through consensual cohabitation than by a formal religious ceremony. By sharing a home with Padi, Maat-Djehuty established herself as "Mistress of the House" in a state of acknowledged equality. The couple shared ownership of their property. As in many societies, a primary aim of their marriage was procreation, a goal fulfilled by the birth of Ankh-Hap in the late fourth century BCE. Padi and Maat-Djehuty apparently achieved no high station about which their offspring could later boast. On his coffin, Ankh-Hap would simply record his parents' names without elaboration, nor would he claim for himself any special title, rank, or profession. Although he lacked notable status, the gilt decoration on his funerary cartonnage indicates some financial success by the end of his life.

As a child, Ankh-Hap suffered from anemia, perhaps associated with malnutrition and disease. He grew older in relatively good health save for developing arthritis in his neck. His first birthday may have been cause for formal celebration since birth and childhood in antiquity were always fraught with danger, even in a nation as medically advanced as Egypt.[13] The practice of mummification afforded the Egyptians millions upon millions of opportunities to study anatomy, thus escaping the taboos that inhibited physicians in other cultures. In fact, the Egyptian word for a doctor (*swnw*) was often applied to an embalmer as well.[14] Egyptian doctors benefited, too, from the detailed corpus of medical papyri that passed down surgical and other techniques to successive generations of trained practitioners. Of course, magic and medicine were not mutually exclusive in the treatment of patients such as Ankh-Hap.[15]

The child was likely raised on a simple diet based heavily upon barley and emmer wheat, supplemented by fruits, beans, garlic, and onions. The grains provided bread and beer, cherished commodities referenced in his coffin inscription; the text's additional appeal for flesh, fowl, wine, and milk aspired to less common fare in the household larder. Some Egyptians owned goats, pigs, and sheep, but meat and dairy products were rare delicacies for most persons lacking the means to stable cattle or to store perishables. For protein, the courtyards of village houses might contain a few pigeons or ducks. The Nile, of course, provided fish and marsh plants as a dietary supplement. Honey was the sweetener of choice, and hives were maintained along the valley on nearly an industrial scale.[16] Cooking often took place outdoors in brick ovens or on stoves, wafting their aromas across each crowded village. Mudbrick homes tended to be quite small and simple. They had narrow windows, dirt floors, and no real plumbing beyond perhaps a latrine. Houses were furnished with stools or chairs, small tables, reed mats, and raised beds to escape whatever crept or crawled. Rats and mice shared most habitations, which accounts for the veneration of cats as human companions. Fleas and other insects flourished everywhere, prompting the Egyptians to include in their medical papyri various recipes for insecticides.

Whatever their living conditions, people of all ranks kept their clothes and bodies as clean as possible. Most Egyptians bathed in the Nile or its canals, using simple homemade soaps. Aromatics, if affordable, freshened the skin and suppressed odors. Cosmetics, oils, and creams were popular with both sexes to combat the ravages of age under the relentless Egyptian sun. Shaving the body was considered necessary for personal hygiene, and wigs were often worn outside the home by women and men. As a young child, Ankh-Hap surely ran about naked; adults of the family donned linen garments, preferring them to be bleached as white as practical. As an adult, Ankh-Hap wore a kilt tied tightly around his waist and reaching nearly to his knees. He normally wore no shirt except for special occasions. Sandals might complete the outfit of the well-dressed Egyptian.

As he matured, Ankh-Hap probably received an informal education at home and later may have been apprenticed to learn a trade. Egyptian civilization relied upon many skilled occupations, from carpenter and scribe to farmer and merchant. Whatever path he followed, Ankh-Hap worked and worshiped his way through life, paying his taxes, doting on the meaning of his dreams as god-sent messages, and dutifully observing the great festivals. He probably took a wife and raised children of his own, but we have no way of knowing these things. Who buried Ankh-Hap, and whom he had buried before him, are lost to us. We can, however, situate his life and death within the larger panorama of a remarkable period in Egypt's long history.

TURBULENT TIMES

Padi, Maat-Djehuty, and Ankh-Hap witnessed the onset of a bril-liant and boisterous new era that we now call the Hellenistic Age (323–30 BCE). This was a direct result of the conquests of young Alexander the Great from faraway Macedonia in northern Greece. Egypt had already suffered through centuries of foreign rule since about 950 BCE when the Twenty-Second Dynasty brought invaders from Libya; these were followed by occupiers from Nubia (Dynasty 25) and Assyria (Dynasty 26). Then the Persian Empire established Dynasty 27, ruling Egypt off and on between 525 and 332 BCE. The alleged indifference of the Persians to Egyptian culture and re-ligion triggered a particularly hostile tradition. In 525, the Persian king Cambyses reportedly ordered the desecration of a pharaoh's mummy, scourging the corpse, pulling out its hair, and then set-ting the body on fire.[17] Cambyses allegedly mocked and then killed the Apis bull in a fit of madness.[18] It was said in Ankh-Hap's day that one of the last of the Persian kings, Artaxerxes III Ochus, had recently recovered Egypt and driven into exile a native Egyptian pharaoh named Nectanebo II; Artaxerxes then slaughtered an-other Apis bull at Memphis before despoiling the local temples in 343 BCE.[19] Thereafter, Egypt remained in turmoil as a native rebel named Khababash raised another revolt against the Persians and claimed the title of pharaoh. Pointedly, Khababash oversaw the burial of an Apis bull, one of only two events attested for his brief reign between about 338 and 336 BCE.[20] Khababash was soon expelled, and Egypt was reabsorbed as a satrapy (province) into the Persian Empire. Within just a few years, however, the Persian king Darius III was battling in Syria the invading army of Alexander the Great. There in 333, Darius lost the Battle of Issus and fled east toward Mesopotamia, leaving Egypt undefended. The Persian satrap (governor) of Egypt had been slain in the battle, adding to the political and military chaos that gripped the Nile valley. Rogue elements took command of local forces to fight each other for the spoils of war, while on the horizon Alexander turned his victorious army south toward Egypt.[21]

Every Egyptian had to make a choice about the future. Unfortunately, only a few left an extant account of their actions, and Ankh-Hap was not one of them. Fortunately, an Egyptian doctor named Semtutefnakht handed down to us a stone funerary memorial describing his personal ordeal. In it, he lamented that the gods had lately forsaken Egypt, probably a common complaint among his contemporaries.[22] Semtutefnakht personally witnessed the awesome power of Alexander's army at the Battle of Issus.[23] There the physician fled from Persian service, believing himself suddenly spared by divine intervention. He returned to Egypt, awaiting the consequences of the Macedonian victory over the crumbling Persian Empire. Semtutefnakht navigated these turbulent waters well, finding it possible to survive, and even to prosper, under the new Macedonian regime. Alexander arrived in 332 BCE as a liberator, founding the city of Alexandria and taking care to honor native traditions. One of his first public acts was to offer sacrifice to the

Apis bull at Memphis.[24] He took pharaonic titles and called himself the "Beloved of Re and chosen of Ammon."[25]

As a result, many Egyptians embraced Alexander as one of their own. Ankh-Hap surely heard the rumors that Alexander's true father was not really King Philip II of Macedonia, but rather the refugee pharaoh Nectanebo himself. This tale involved a magical transformation of Nectanebo into a serpent so that he could impregnate Olympias, one of Philip's wives, and so conceive in Macedonia a deliverer for Egypt.[26] Egyptian folklore refashioned Alexander the foreigner into a local hero. Alexander thereby became ruler of Egypt by right as well as by might, or so some proud Egyptians preferred to believe.[27] They found solace in the fiction that young Alexander had professed to the world, "I am the son of an Egyptian father."[28]

A few years later, the unexpected death of Alexander at Babylon in 323 BCE unleashed the ambitions of his generals, among whom a boyhood friend named Ptolemy seized Egypt. He founded a Macedonian dynasty there that would endure for nearly three centuries (305–30 BCE). To legitimize his reign, Ptolemy hijacked the body of Alexander and brought it to Egypt for burial. He then glorified his role in Alexander's conquests by writing a history of their exploits together. He also followed Alexander's lead by continuing the building of Alexandria in Egypt as a showcase city of science, culture, and cosmopolitanism. King Ptolemy depicted himself both as a Macedonian monarch and an Egyptian pharaoh. He may have inventoried the royal tombs of Egypt, since it was recorded by the priests of his day that only fifteen remained.[29] Ptolemy even loaned a huge sum of money worth over twenty-eight hundred pounds of silver for the burial of an Apis bull.[30] The king also promoted a popular Greco-Egyptian deity called Serapis that combined the Apis cult with that of Osiris, the Egyptian god of the Underworld whom the Greeks identified as their own Hades.

No one knows exactly what Ankh-Hap, or millions of other Egyptians, thought of these events. Scholars today argue vigorously whether natives and newcomers embraced, or even understood, each other's culture. Did the Greco-Macedonians and Egyptians assimilate, segregate, collaborate, or quarrel? Despite the conciliatory pronouncements and posturing of Alexander and the Ptolemies, did the mass of Greco-Macedonian soldiers and settlers in Egypt conduct themselves as swaggering conquerors entitled to the spoils of war? Did they prosper at the expense of the native population? Were the locals angry at the changes being imposed upon them, such as a foreign monetary economy that favored Greek coins rather than wheat and other commodities to pay rents, settle debts, and meet new taxation demands? Were the Egyptians offended to see the Greco-Macedonians engaged in cultural and religious appropriation, such as Ptolemy dressing as a pharaoh and meddling in their cults? Whatever Ankh-Hap himself felt about these changes, he carried those thoughts and the age-old name of Apis with him to the grave.

THE NEXT LIFE BEGINS

The remarkable journey taken by Ankh-Hap from Ptolemaic Egypt to modern Texas began with an ironic valediction: family and friends spoke of his death as "going West" with the setting sun. Before he could depart, however, skilled embalmers must busily transform his body into a *sah*, something the immigrant Greeks loosely described as *tarichos* ("salted meat") or *soma heilismenon* ("a wrapped-up person").[31] Today we call this a mummy, from a medieval misunderstanding of the Arabic word *mumiyah*, a kind of bitumen sometimes associated with the mummification process.[32] Writing out the name and wrapping the preserved body were essential for a good life to be lived again, not in an ethereal and unfamiliar new realm but rather in a sort of uber-Egypt that looked very much like home. There the reanimated mummy could eat, drink, and even be sexually active in the next life.

The existence of an Egyptian as a person, on either side of death, required the union of a physical body, a birth name, a *Ba*, and a *Ka*. Ancient concepts such as *Ba* and *Ka* are difficult to define, and therefore many Egyptologists prefer not to suggest a modern translation, but in practical terms the *Ba* denotes a personality and the *Ka* a life force. These are elements of what we might lump together into our conception of an eternal spirit. The key point is that any notion of a soul shedding the human body as useless cargo in the afterlife was anathema in ancient Egypt. To be, or not to be, depended in part upon the preservation of the name along with the corpse. Burying both together would provide an identifiable repository for Ankh-Hap's *Ba* and *Ka*, and this would guarantee eternal life—or so his mourners wished. As they gathered to recite prayers and sing songs about the journey he was about to begin, they had no idea how horribly their hopes would be betrayed over the following millennia. They would be appalled at what we would see in our CT scan, for the venerable Egyptian *Book of Going Forth by Day* (sometimes inaccurately called the *Book of the Dead*) entitled the deceased to proclaim:

> I shall possess my body forever. I shall not be corrupted. I shall not disintegrate, nor fall prey to worms. I exist. I am alive. I am strong. I have wakened and am at peace. There is no destruction of my organs or eyes. My head has not been removed from my neck.[33]

Somewhere in Ptolemaic Egypt, family and friends cried out lamentations and smeared themselves with mud to display their grief. They made a crowd-gathering commotion as they carried the fresh corpse to the guild of local priests in charge of embalming.[34] The ministrations of these professionals were deeply religious and as much a performance as a pragmatic effort to preserve the recognizable remains of Ankh-Hap. Mummification had been practiced in Egypt for thousands of years, with priests experimenting and perfecting their craft while observing elaborate rituals (Figure 2.3). Some embalmers, of course, did their jobs differently than others, and some clients were constrained by costs from enjoying excess finery. The most expensive mummification process could take seventy days of preparation and required substantial quantities of expensive materials such as cinnamon, frankincense, myrrh, cassia, palm wine, oils, gum arabic, rolls of linen, and lots of natron

Figure 2.3. Mummification in Egypt
Source: Vladimir Melnik / Shutterstock.com.

(a naturally occurring desiccant resembling a mixture of salt and baking soda). A pricelist of materials was supplied, from which the family could select according to their means.[35]

These costs were meant to offset the unpleasant realities of death and decomposition.[36] After all, it is what does not happen after death that makes a mummy a mummy. Nature generously supplies the myriad elements that together constitute a living entity, but eventually nature wants all of it back. That debt comes due within seconds of death, and it is repaid through the relentless processes of organic decomposition. While death may strike a body with the blunt force of a wrecking ball—a war wound, perhaps, or a fatal disease—the means by which nature then breaks down and reclaims that body are more focused and refined. They are precise, patient, and predictable. It starts with the same little catalytic engines that a moment before had made life possible: enzymes. Once the heart stops pumping blood, cells deprived of oxygen trigger a biochemical reaction. Cellular membranes break down as enzymes quickly turn against their host. They begin digesting the body from the inside out in a process called autolysis. Those parts of the body endowed in life with larger shares of these devourers will naturally autolyze first, such as the liver and intestines, where these enzymes had earlier been dining on harmful bacteria.

Ambient heat helps fuel the spreading feast, making the hot climate of Egypt especially favorable for this intestinal foraging unless mummification intervenes. Otherwise, a loosening of the skin and changes in the cadaver's coloration soon signal other things happening inside. Within half an hour, gravity begins to pool the stagnant blood (*livor mortis*), discoloring the skin in telltale patterns reflecting the positioning of the body. After a few hours, first in the face and jaw and later in the limbs, the depletion of a molecule called adenosine triphosphate causes the muscles to stiffen (*rigor mortis*). After a day or so, the tautened muscle fibers succumb to the feast, relaxing the body once more.

Meanwhile, if not interrupted, the millions of microbial diners intent upon devouring the body keep belching out noxious gases that will inflate the corpse to nearly twice its normal size. In three to five days, this mounting pressure swells the tongue and bulges the glazed eyes until the body bursts. The cadaver turns green, then red and black. Through openings in the ruptured corpse, a wafting stench invites other guests to the banquet according to a guest list carefully prepared by nature. First to arrive are the buzzing flies, summoned from a mile or more away. Blowflies, houseflies, and flesh flies settle upon moist openings in the body such as nostrils, eyes, mouth, and wounds. Their eggs soon hatch into squirming maggots, which then entice rove and clown beetles to feed. Ants may arrive as well. The remaining soft tissues liquefy, leaving behind a residue of hair, bone, and cartilage. Dermestid beetles devour the last remaining flesh so thoroughly that museum curators and taxidermists use them to prepare skeletons for display. Last on the guestlist are centipedes, millipedes, snails, and cockroaches that might find a few leftovers in the surrounding soil. Eventually, the exposed skeleton itself may be gnawed down by larger scavengers as nature reclaims and recycles the last of us.

The purpose of Egyptian mummification was to interdict this irreversible process at a fairly early stage, although in some cases a delay of several days was intentional in order to render a fresh corpse less attractive to necrophiliac embalmers.[37] Inevitably, bodies undergo at least some autolysis before measures can be taken to slow or stop the process. Embalming in modern America was uncommon until the nineteenth century and was only meant to preserve a corpse long enough for transport and burial. Formaldehyde and wood alcohol became the chemicals of choice, injected into the flushed circulatory system to inhibit putrefaction. The ancient Egyptians worked in a different way.

Inside the embalmers' workshop (*wbt*, "the place of purification"), the first step was to extract Ankh-Hap's brain (excerebration). This could be accomplished by punching through the foramen magnum at the base of the skull, but the priests chose the more common practice of inserting a long metal or wooden probe up the nose, breaking through the ethmoid bone to the brain, and scrambling this organ as if beating eggs with a whisk.[38] The resulting slurry could then be drained back through the nostrils and discarded. An ancient Egyptian's brain was the only major part of the deceased's body to be tossed aside as waste.[39] Today, we hold the brain in particularly high regard because it is the locus of our most intimate selves: our thoughts, personality, emotions, self-awareness, and dreams. For the ancient Egyptians, however, those essential attributes resided not in the head but in the heart, based on their everyday experiences. Whether agitated, aroused, nervous, or calm, their beating hearts—not their brains—mirrored all their moods. Thus, Egyptians were usually embalmed with their hearts left in place, there to be judged in the afterlife as the arbiter of all their actions. The brain was deemed useless in this respect, and it posed an imminent threat in the embalmers' fight against their natural enemy—putrefaction. Because brains rot quickly, they were best removed right away, and the cranium flushed with unguents and filled with aromatic resins. After just days with the embalmers, Ankh-Hap lay as brainless as Dorothy's Scarecrow but with the heart wanting in the Tin Woodsman. Stretched there on the embalming slab, his head was tilted slightly to the left as the resin hardened in his skull. That glass-like substance shows brightly in the CT scan images, pooled to one side, taking us back to that very day when Ankh-Hap began his transformation.

Next, the guild of undertakers took care of the viscera. They harvested the deceased's organs, not for the living as we sometimes do today, but to be given back to the dead. Using a sharp obsidian blade from Ethiopia, a special worker designated the "Slitter" (called a *paraschistes* by the Greeks)[40] made an incision into the left abdominal flank. Because this necessary action violated the corpse, the "Slitter" was ritually chased from the premises by his "angry" colleague, the "Preserver" (in Greek, the *taricheutes*),[41] who then could safely care for the stomach, liver, lungs, and intestines. These organs were carefully preserved and kept with the body, either in special containers called canopic jars or packed as bundles within the body. None of these was still with Ankh-Hap when he arrived in Houston.

Next, the empty body cavity was cleansed with palm wine and then treated with aromatic spices and natron. The former deodorized the corpse, and the latter dehydrated it over the course of many weeks. To maintain a body's shape, it was often packed with scraps of linen and other materials such as mud, straw, or sawdust. Ankh-Hap's mourners might have chosen less costly options by not surgically removing the viscera at all. For example, embalmers could inject a body with cedar oil through the anus, which was then plugged. This would eventually liquefy the internal organs, allowing them to be drained away when the stopper was removed. The corpse could then be dried with natron.

Mummies, of course, must all be wrapped using rituals no less elaborate or important than any other in the preparations for an afterlife.[42] The linen bandages themselves were steeped in magic and helped to protect the person or animal concealed inside them. Workers called *wetiu* ("bandagers") wound the wrappings from head to foot, accompanied by prayers and anointing. The venerated

Figure 2.4. Tattered cartonnage on the mummy of Ankh-Hap

result could then be decorated with panels of painted cartonnage, sometimes gilt, as was the case for Ankh-Hap (Figure 2.4).

When fully wrapped and ready, the mummy of Ankh-Hap was placed inside its protective coffin.[43] The elaborate designs on this painted wooden box read like an illustrated manual of Egyptian mortuary cult, with a host of funerary deities taking their posts around the body. Soon the coffin and its contents were retrieved by the family and hauled in its painted coffin to the grave. This might be done by dragging the load on a skid pulled by oxen, surrounded by wailing mourners who might include professionals paid for their grieving. The highlight of the funeral was the "Opening of the Mouth" ceremony that enabled the mummy to breathe, eat, and speak. A coterie of priests performed this purification rite and held special implements to the mummy's eyes and mouth; one of these tools was a knife representing the blade that cuts the umbilical cord when a person first comes to eat and breathe on its own. This reanimated the corpse in that comforting cycle of birth-death-rebirth that so satisfied the Egyptian psyche. Brought magically back to life, the mummy joined the funeral party in a final above-ground banquet before being settled into its tomb.

Things, of course, could sometimes go wrong. What happened if a complete body could not be delivered to the embalmers? In those instances, special rituals were observed and the corpse was repaired lest the victim lack an arm or a leg in the afterlife. Missing body parts were sometimes replaced with substitutes made of mud, sticks, or even animal bones. This happened, too, when arms or legs went astray during the long mummification process. Limbs were known to fall loose after rough handling or excessive drying by the priests; some were lost in the scatter of bodies being embalmed, or they were dragged off by hungry jackals lurking nearby. These creatures fed on carrion and thus found embalming tents and graveyards quite attractive haunts. As a result, the association of jackals with mummification became extraordinarily powerful. Anubis, the Egyptian god of embalming, took the form of a jackal-headed man.

What had made mummification such an important part of Egyptian culture? Replicating the myth and magic of Osiris was paramount.[44] According to legend, the benevolent king Osiris ruled earliest Egypt with his sister/wife Isis at his side. Osiris had two other siblings, his jealous brother Seth and another sister named Nephthys, who were married to each other as a second divine pair. To be rid of Osiris, Seth put in motion a devious plan involving an ornate chest shaped like a man. Osiris was challenged to fit himself into the chest, which allowed Seth to quickly seal it shut. Thus trapped, Osiris was tossed into the Nile, and his body floated far beyond Egypt to Lebanon. Inconsolable, the devoted Isis searched the earth until she found the box and brought it back home. Seth, now governing the land as its supreme ruler, responded by angrily chopping up the salvaged body of Osiris and scattering its parts across the length and breadth of Egypt.

Isis and her sister Nephthys hunted down every piece of their dismembered brother Osiris, save one—his procreative penis. It had been eaten by a Nile fish, so with the help of Anubis they fashioned a fake one and attached it to the reassembled body of their brother. Thus did Osiris become the prototypical mummy. Restored and resurrected, Osiris impregnated Isis. Their son, falcon-headed Horus, avenged his father and replaced Seth as lord of the living while Osiris henceforth ruled the land of the dead. Accordingly, Osiris appears in Egyptian art as a white mummy, often with a green face since that color symbolized resurrection. Thereafter, death in Egypt meant transforming into Osiris as a mummy inside its coffin. This was no mere slumber, for the dead were alive so long as they were endowed with their birth name, body, *Ba*, and *Ka*. In fact, the *Ba* could fly like a bird between the realms of Horus and Osiris, visiting back and forth for eternity. It must, however, be able to recognize and return to the mummified body without which it could not exist.[45]

The finality of physical death felt so strongly in other cultures had no hold over the Egyptians. Theirs was no obsession with death, but with life. Whereas other cultures might lock the door behind the dearly departed, the Egyptians left the door ajar. Passing freely between the worlds of the living and dead, Ankh-Hap the man continued his life's journey as Ankh-Hap the mummy. He would be judged before a tribunal of the gods who demanded an accounting of all his earthly actions. He must deny dozens of specific transgressions: "I have not killed . . . stolen . . . lied . . . cheated . . . committed adultery . . . mistreated slaves . . . poached . . . disrupted irrigation" and so on. To swear falsely would weigh heavily upon his heart, an evil revealed to all when Anubis placed that heart upon the scales of justice. A feather of Maat, goddess of cosmic harmony, would be weighed against the mummy's heart; failure to measure up meant tossing that organ into the hungry jaws of a horrible beast called Ammit the Devourer (Figure 2.5). This hybrid creature (part crocodile, lioness, and hippopotamus) destroyed the personhood of the deceased and ended all hopes for eternal life. A successful judgment, however, rendered the righteous into an *Akh*, or resurrected self that had been duly justified. This ghostly *Akh* could interact with the living and might be petitioned for help through prayers or even letters left in cemeteries; on the other hand, an angry *Akh* might haunt those who had injured or neglected them.[46]

There is so much to admire about the rituals and beliefs of the ancient Egyptians. Their version of reality projects an inherent optimism and calm that is worthy of continued study. They pined not for pearly gates, heavenly mansions, and streets of gold, but for the Egypt they already knew and loved. Their alternate fate was not an eternity spent burning in hell, but instead a lamented state of

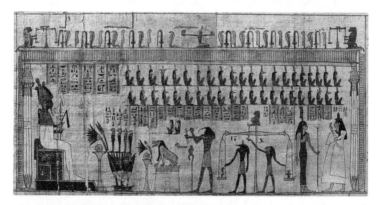

Figure 2.5. Weighing-of-the-heart ceremony
Source: Kriveart90 / Shutterstock.com.

nonexistence. Each Egyptian wanted to endure as a unified self, but for some, all the preparations and precautions in the world could not safeguard them. The unfortunate Ankh-Hap must be counted among them.

AN AFTERLIFE INTERRUPTED

The first disturbance of Ankh-Hap's afterlife may have occurred within just a thousand years of his burial. Some of the cloth that wrapped loose bones in his coffin was carbon-dated to the early centuries CE. As with Manchester mummy 1770, this suggested to us that the body of Ankh-Hap had been despoiled and then rewrapped in Roman times. After the reigns of more than a dozen Ptolemies, Egypt had been annexed as a Roman province when Queen Cleopatra VII died in the custody of Octavian, soon to be Rome's first emperor, in 30 BCE. For centuries thereafter, the verdant Nile valley fed the city of Rome and adorned its plazas with obelisks and other monuments seized as potent symbols of conquest. Immigrant Romans settled among the Egyptians and Greco-Macedonians, and many joined them in the afterlife as mummies.[47] All of them were fair game for the ubiquitous scourge of grave robbers.

Looting tombs was not the oldest profession in Egypt, but it may have been the earliest moonlighting job in both senses of the word. Tradesmen from masons to musicians sometimes supplemented their daytime earnings by digging at night into graves. They stole valuables such as amulets and jewelry that were cached inside the tombs or hidden within the mummies' wrappings. Why would people so steeped in the sacred rites of mummification and burial dare to ransack tombs? The answer lies not in a crisis of faith, but of finances. While many would never consider committing such atrocities, there were always some whose need or greed made irresistible the wealth awaiting them underground.

The richest spoils had come, of course, from royal tombs, but these ventures also carried the greatest risks. Ancient court records detail the investigations of looted pharaonic tombs.[48] The trials typically relied upon confessions extracted through torture; the guilty were then gruesomely impaled through the anus. Robbers nevertheless entered the tombs of all the pharaohs, including the so-called unlooted grave of Tutankhamun that was actually violated soon after his burial. The evidence is quite clear that necropolis officials tidied and resealed his sepulchre following these crimes.

Tomb raiding occurred in all periods of Egyptian history, but the problem was particularly acute from the thirteenth century BCE onward. Scholars have concluded: "Down to the end of antiquity, even the most modest tombs fell victim to pillaging."[49] Thus, long after the Ptolemaic dynasty had ended, thieves apparently found and ransacked the grave of Ankh-Hap. Any precious objects wrapped with his body were probably lost at that time; certainly, none remained to be detected by our CT scan. When the ancient priests hurriedly rewrapped what they could recover of him, the bones in their loose bundles show that the body of Ankh-Hap had been severely damaged and disarticulated. It is unlikely, however, that these caretakers inserted any of the wooden poles that now brace the mummy, since at least one of these is unmistakably modern.

To whatever extent Ankh-Hap was able to resume his disrupted afterlife following this traumatic experience, more tribulations were yet to come. Mummies were never safe in any era. They were relentlessly plundered by those seeking wealth, and eventually by others seeking health. In early Arab medicine, the word *mumiyah* meant the dark bituminous mineral pitch highly valued for the treatment of illness and injury. Knowledge of its healing properties spread to Europe, particularly during the Crusades. Supplies of natural bitumen were limited, however, and increasing demand facilitated a series of misunderstandings and mistranslations that finally equated *mumiyah* with the blackened bodies of embalmed Egyptians. Thus, the pervasive use of mummies for medicinal purposes created a devastating demand for the dead of ancient Egypt.[50] In apothecary shops around the world, *mumia vera aegyptiaca* denoted the curative powder of crushed Egyptian corpses.[51] Pulverized mummies were widely valued as a panacea for the treatment of abscesses, fractures, rheumatism, epilepsy, dizziness, nausea, ulcers, heart ailments, coughs, poisoning, and other maladies.[52] Early chemists and apothecaries discussed Egyptian mummies alongside such creatures as unicorns as a source of drugs.[53] The physician Guy de la Fontaine traveled to Egypt in the sixteenth century to find out more about mummies and healing. He later accused Jews in Alexandria of establishing a medicinal trade in ancient mummies and then hiking profits by substituting contemporary dead bodies for the real thing. He reported the confessions of one such dealer:

> as to the Dead he took such Bodies as he could get, whether they dy'd of a common Disease, or of some Contagion . . . which after he had dry'd in an Oven he sent into Europe; and that he was amaz'd to see the Christians were Lovers of such Filthiness.[54]

The trafficking of dead bodies deeply troubled some antiquarians such as Sir Thomas Browne, who complained: "The Aegyptian mummies, which Cambyses or time hath spared, avarice now consumeth. Mummie is become Merchandise."[55] Likewise, a line in

James Shirley's 1633 play *The Bird in a Cage* laments: "make mummy of my flesh, and sell me to the apothecaries."[56] Even centuries later, a doctor in New York could scarcely convince his patients to take proper medicines because they insisted upon swallowing a miracle cure-all of ground-up mummies still containing identifiable bits of bone and cuticle.[57] The German pharmaceutical giant Merck still sold *mumia vera aegyptiaca* by the kilogram as late as 1924.[58] People even believed they could be cured by association. It was reported in 1881 that putting a mummy's hand under the left armpit was a remedy for fever, and that childless women venturing into the Egyptian mummy-pits would be guaranteed the birth of a healthy son.[59]

Not all mummies were valued equally for their medicinal efficacy. An encyclopedic reference work of the early modern period, the *Grete Herball*, advised its readers: "That mommye is to be chosen that is bryght blacke stynkynge and styffe."[60] This English guidebook warned against using a mummy that was powdery or poorly tinted. The Italian traveler Pietro della Valle advised in 1616 that the mummies of maidens and virgins were the most effective for healing the sick and injured.[61] Also highly valued were the potent bodies of ancient royals. The poet Richard Savage wrote in 1780:

> From Egypt thus a rival traffic springs,
> Her vended mummies thus were once her kings.[62]

Royal mummies might even be consumed as a powerful aphrodisiac, if the poem "Mummia" (1911) by Rupert Brooke can be believed:

> As those of old drank mummia
> To fire their limbs of lead,

Making dead kings from Africa
Stand pandar to their bed;
Drunk on the dead, and medicined
With spiced imperial dust,
In a short night they reeled to find
Ten centuries of lust.

Brooke himself confessed to a mummy fetish so passionate that he dreamed of stealing at night into the British Museum to cuddle with one of its Egyptian corpses.[63]

As more than just a drug, mummies became part of some people's diets. The German physician Johann Blumenbach in 1794 commented upon reports of eating mummies at the dinner table.[64] In 1839, a reviewer of French cuisine noted, "Some of the science-association-gentlemen taste mummy I know, and dare say it is relishing."[65] Fish apparently liked it, too. Anglers in the seventeenth century developed a fish-bait recipe with mummies as an ingredient:

Boil clean Water, then put Barley into it, when it bursts: then put Liquorice, a little Mummy and some Honey, and beat them to-gether in a Mortar into a stiff Paste, and boil about the Quantity of a large Nutmeg of this Paste, with a Quart of Barley, till it grows like Glew, then lay it for ground bait, and all the Fish will come to it.[66]

Entrepreneurs profited from the linen bandages as well as the bodies wrapped inside them. One German opportunist raided Egyptian tombs on an industrial scale:

[He] employed men to bring out the mummies wholesale; he stripped off their bandages, and freighted a large barge with them as rags for the paper mills; the bones of men and reptiles alike he carried off to make superphosphate of, so that the poor Egyptians who took such pains to find a resting-place where they might never be disturbed, have been applied as manure to the ground, and will be eaten in the shape of bread grown from this strangely compounded superphosphate. Such is life and such is death![67]

A nineteenth-century shortage of rags from which to manufacture paper had put a premium on mummy wrappings, which meant that mummies were destroyed indiscriminately.[68] The idea of exploiting Egypt's mummy-pits for this purpose appealed to many capitalists who calculated the immense profits down to the dollar. According to a notice in *Scientific American* (June 19, 1847, p. 309):

> Mehemet Ali has found a new source of revenue, in the fine linen in which the immense deposits of mummies are wrapped, by applying it to the manufacture of paper. Calculations, founded upon mummy statistics, make the linen swathings of the ancient Egyptians worth $21,000,006.

This same Mehemet Ali (Muhammad Ali Pasha) was also accused of burning mummies to fuel the trains of Egypt:

> Some years ago, owing to threatened exhaustion of the stock of mummies, already depleted by Mehemet Ali's reckless use of them as fuel for his locomotives, the Egyptian government prohibited the exportation of mummies from the country.[69]

It was probably Mark Twain who created as a joke the notion of mummy-fueled locomotives, writing in *The Innocents Abroad*

(1869): "sometimes one hears the profane engineer call out pettishly, "D——n these plebeians, they don't burn worth a cent— pass out a King.""[70] Another American wag spun the tale of an extract of Egyptian mummy, bottled and sold to bald customers as a hair restorer and as a dye for those turning gray.[71]

Hair dye, paper, fuel, and fertilizer were among the least alarming of these byproducts, rumors notwithstanding of a cholera epidemic caused by New England butchers who wrapped their meats in parcels of mummy paper.[72] In 1874, American newspapers spread the word that a popular pancake syrup, Golden Drip, was being made using rags stripped from Egyptian mummies:

> There is trouble in the minds of people, for adulteration in its worst form has been discovered. The father of the family, as he poured the rich syrup over his buckwheats at breakfast, and gave of the same to the wife of his bosom and the child of his heart, little dreamed that he was giving them poison and a most disgusting poison at that.[73]

Artists put demands on the mummy trade as well. Beginning in the Renaissance, a thriving market existed among painters and dyers for ground-up mummies. In Shakespeare's *Othello* (Act 3, Scene 4), Desdemona's ill-fated handkerchief "was dyed in mummy" using the pure hearts of macerated maidens. In 1903, the *New York Tribune* printed photographs of factory workers in Philadelphia grinding up mummies and filling tubes with the resulting pigment; a beautiful, emptied coffin stands nearby.[74] The accompanying story relates:

> Every large dealer in oil paints sells powdered mummy, and almost every manufacturer of pigments has a mummy department,

where, in a spice-laden atmosphere, amid surroundings pictur-
esque and grewsome, young men and women grind up the dried
bodies of Egyptian princesses and priests, mix the powder with
poppy oil and bottle it for the market in little tubes of tin.

Defending his business, the proprietor extols the artwork enhanced
by his company's product and states:

I buy my mummies through a dealer in Paris. Where he gets his
stock I don't know, but he is never at a loss to fill an order. . . . A big
factory like ours will buy a whole mummy at a time. A smaller one
will buy a body, a leg or a couple of arms.

In 1908, a Texas newspaper in a town where Ankh-Hap would later
reside commented, "It makes one shudder to think of the sacrilege
of grinding the mummy of some ancient Egyptian king into powder
to be used as a pigment."[75] Nevertheless, as late as 1964, *Time* magazine carried a story about a London company that manufactured
Mummy Brown from ancient corpses; the managing director of
the firm was quoted: "We might have a few odd limbs lying around
somewhere, but not enough to make any more paint. We sold our
last complete mummy some years ago for, I think, £3."[76] Later in
my investigations, I was fated to learn more about the macabre mer-
chandising of mummy limbs.

Mummy Brown was so popular that many canvases on display
in our finest museums have been daubed with the bodies of dead
Egyptians. For example, it is believed that the iconic 1830 painting
Liberty Leading the People by Eugène Delacroix, now in the Louvre,
was produced with this pigment. Some artists were unaware that
their paints were infused with powdered mummies, a revelation that

hit a few consciences especially hard. In 1881, when Edward Burne-Jones learned the horrible truth about Mummy Brown, he

> hastened to the studio, and returning with the only tube he had, insisted on our giving it decent burial there and then. So a hole was bored in the green grass at our feet, and we all watched it put safely in, and the spot was marked by one of the girls planting a daisy root above it.[77]

It is possible, of course, that these industrial and dietary uses of mummies were less widespread and profitable than might appear from the press and other anecdotal sources.[78] Yet notices in newspapers and magazines that we might question today were nevertheless powerful and believable at the time, capable of spreading a covetous and capitalist interest in mummies and their wrappings. After all, most of what the average American once knew about mummies depended upon the press, which published thousands of items with headlines and bylines sure to arouse popular interest such as "CLEOPATRA'S BONES FOR $60,000" or "MUMMY WORKS EVIL SPELL."[79] More people in nineteenth- and early twentieth-century America perused newspapers than visited museums or read books about Egyptology, which inspired the reception of mummies as raw materials rather than as human beings.

While some missing parts of Ankh-Hap's body may have been reduced to fertilizer, fish food, paper, paint, or medicine, the ramming of a modern stick down his neck to keep his head in place points to another fate. Almost certainly in the nineteenth century, his tomb was disturbed again and his mummy sent to America to serve someone as a showpiece. Ankh-Hap was not the first, the last, nor the most unfortunate to suffer this kind of abuse, as I was destined to discover.

Chapter 3

Coming to America

Walk in and see the mummies, ladies and gentlemen, the most wonderful mummies ever found!

—Barker at the Chicago World's Fair, 1893[1]

MUMMIES MAKING MONEY

Before his death, Ankh-Hap surely anticipated the possible looting
of his tomb by contemporary treasure-seekers, but could he have
imagined that people might someday profit by displaying corpses
like his to the paying public? Monetizing mummies as corporeal
curiosities is a peculiar phenomenon, fraught with ethical concerns.
While few people today would approve of damaging or destroying
mummies for any purpose, opinions vary widely about putting
human bodies on public display. The British Museum, for example,
holds more than six thousand human remains in its collections,
ranging from shrunken heads and trophy skulls to cremations
and, of course, mummies.[2] Many of these remains are openly displayed, governed sometimes by the competing interests of museum
administrators, British lawmakers, and the public at large.[3] Not sur-
prisingly, the gallery of Egyptian mummies is the most visited space

in the vast British Museum, proving just how keenly its patrons want to see these ancient bodies firsthand (Figure 3.1).[4]

The role of museums has been closely scrutinized in recent years, some critics arguing that they are vestiges of colonial exploitation, while others defend the right—even the responsibility—to share with patrons the materials in their care, including human remains.[5] The Egyptian government itself has long wrestled with this issue, sometimes displaying its cache of royal mummies, and then withholding them again from public view whenever sentiments have wavered. In April 2021, an elaborate public procession transported twenty-two royal mummies from their display cases in the old Egyptian Museum in Tahrir Square to the new Royal Mummies Hall, crown jewel of the National Museum of Egyptian Civilization in Fustat. The multi-million-dollar parade included singers, dancers, and dignitaries who escorted each of the mummies in its own

Figure 3.1. Mummies displayed in the British Museum
Source: Tupungato / Shutterstock.com.

ornate vehicle through the streets of Cairo.[6] The event has been commemorated and commercialized with special coins (Figure 3.2) and stamps intended to capture national pride, although some Egyptians have decried the spectacle as religiously and culturally offensive.

Simply put, who decides? Do the ancient dead have any rights? Is it possible to guess on behalf of an Amenhotep or an Ankh-Hap whether those individuals would want their mummies studied and displayed, as some suggest we try to determine?[7] How should we comply with a mummy's imagined wishes—by keeping the body locked away in storage, returning it to the cave or grave from which it came, or carving it up in the anatomy lab? Even the exceptional replacement of Tutankhamun's dismembered body back in

Figure 3.2. Coin commemorating The Pharaohs' Golden Parade, 2021

his emptied tomb does not conform to the wishes of his ancient mourners. The pharaoh lies today in a much-trampled space bereft of the possessions once deemed essential for his proper burial. Many of those treasures keep circling the globe in lucrative museum exhibitions, lost to Tut, but no more so than the grave-goods of all the other pharaohs whose tombs were thoroughly pillaged in antiquity. Molesting mummies is a millennial problem, and profit is nearly always the motive.

A SIGHT TO BEHOLD

Only half in jest, I tell my students that Napoleon Bonaparte was often portrayed with one hand thrust inside his shirt because there he was hiding something stolen from an Egyptian tomb. After all, his invasion of Egypt in 1798 opened wide the eyes and wallets of westerners to the immense spoils awaiting them down in the mummy-pits of the Nile.[8] Napoleon's savants researched and published the wonders of Egypt, inspiring a modern wave of Egyptomania yet to be exhausted.[9] Statues, inscriptions, monuments, and mummies were the spoils of war, seized from Egypt by Napoleon and as quickly snatched from the French by the British. Thus did the famous Rosetta Stone, a key to deciphering the hieroglyphic script, end up in London rather than Paris. Europe's interest in all things Egyptian was matched by new levels of access to its antiquities, especially through the agency of entrepreneurial looters such as Giovanni Belzoni, Henry Salt, and Bernardino Drovetti.[10] The profits of plundering Egypt would eventually attract some American businessman as well.

In the United States, pre-Napoleonic interest in mummies was mostly confined to the passive curiosity of intellectuals such as

Benjamin Franklin.[11] In 1823, however, an Egyptian mummy named Padihershef arrived in America with public acclaim and boundless commercial prospects.[12] An enterprising merchant named Jacob van Lennep had acquired Padihershef and his coffin in Thebes; he gave both to Boston's Massachusetts General Hospital as a means of raising funds.[13] Visitors paid twenty-five cents each to see the "lady" mummy, which would eventually be identified as a male.[14] The first $200 of the proceeds were dedicated to the dispensary and the rest to the hospital.[15] After just a few months, the trustees of Massachusetts General Hospital voted to rent out their lucrative mummy to other cities, such as New York, Philadelphia, Richmond, Charleston, and Augusta. These successful ventures prompted Rubens Peale in May 1824 to arrange an exhibition of Padihershef's mummy and coffin in Baltimore, where the body was still presumed to be that of a princess.[16] In just under six weeks, Peale took in $2,502, one quarter at a time.[17] Meanwhile, the Massachusetts General Hospital profited $650 from the deal, and others made money printing handbills and tickets, running ads for the exhibitors, publishing pamphlets, and providing other necessary support for the wandering one-mummy show.[18]

During this same period, the New England press announced the arrival of a second mummy on American shores, also presumed to be a princess "who appears to be somewhat older than the young lady in Baltimore, having a few grey hairs here and there upon her head."[19] More mummies inevitably followed, prompting several newspapers to report: "The market is already glutted; a few more of these Egyptian carcasses, with a mermaid or two, and the stock of our museums will be as cheap as the candidates for the presidency."[20] In 1829, a lawsuit for wrongful damages was brought against eight men in Rensselaer County, New York, for the lost revenues of an Egyptian mummy, which had been abducted from a public house and dissected by medical students during its exhibition tour.[21] The defendants' counsel argued that this criminal mischief was intended as an act of public service, to establish whether the mummy was genuine or fake; that failing, it was alleged that owning human bodies was immoral and that even a dead person should not have been treated as property. Next, the lawyer claimed that only the surviving family of the mummy could bring suit; and finally, that the corpse was worthless anyway. The plaintiffs successfully countered that the mummy had been producing a net profit of eight dollars a day, and so the jury awarded them $1,200 plus court costs.

Mummies and their coffins toured America as sights to behold in an otherwise workaday world. Newspaper stringers in the nineteenth century thumbed their thesauri tirelessly to convey the exoticism and excitement of these ancient remains, usually to paying customers:

What visions that world conjures up. What ages roll back as we look upon those wonderfully preserved faces and think of the time when they, too, like ourselves of the present day, moved and lived and had their being, when they walked their little day upon the earth, and loved and hated, schemed and planned, joyed and suffered in much the same fashion as we moderns.[22]

The Quaker poet Bernard Barton, inspired by a quarter's worth of curiosity, penned these lines to a mummy seen on exhibition:

Since first thy form was in this box extended,
We have, above ground, seen some strange mutations;
The Roman Empire has begun and ended;
New worlds have risen—we have lost old nations,
And countless kings have into dust been humbled,
While not a fragment of thy flesh has crumbled.[23]

Year by year, demands on the dead of ancient Egypt increased exponentially, rousting mummies out of their tombs in order to display them in store windows, saloons, museums, historical societies, family parlors, world's fairs, circuses, seminaries, lecture halls, and tea parties. In 1859, Jeremiah George Harris of the US Navy purchased a load of Egyptian mummies during his travels and donated the best of them to the Tennessee Historical Society because "nearly all our historical societies have one."[24] Charles F. Gunther, the confectioner who invented Cracker Jack, lured customers to his Chicago store by displaying the mummy of an alleged princess upstairs, alongside the bludgeoned skin of the very snake that had tempted Eve and which Adam had dutifully killed the next day.[25] Gunther claimed his "princess" was none other than the Egyptian who saved Moses from the bulrushes, a popular backstory for many of the mummies brought to America.

Advertisers adored mummies. In 1901, William S. McJimsey exhibited a mummy at his store in Graham, Texas. Anyone spending a dollar or more on merchandise was entitled to view the body, with the proviso, "If you trade less than a dollar, call for a mummy coupon."[26] The second-place prize in a 1911 poetry contest in Tacoma, Washington, went to an entry that begins: "If you're worried or sad with things breaking bad, / And you feel like a clothing store mummy."[27] Merchants made such a habit of luring customers by displaying mummies in their windows that a single body might be rented out to store after store from New York to Nebraska.[28] I was later to discover that in 1929 a piece of cloth taken from Ankh-Hap's mummy was displayed in a downtown store window of the small east Texas town of Liberty.[29]

In the early days of so-called dime museums, the ubiquitous low-cost alternatives to big-city institutions, mummies were a common feature. In one instance, railyards from Paris in east Texas to Big Spring in west Texas treated residents to a traveling spectacle that included an Egyptian mummy variously billed as "the only unwrapped mummy ever brought to America" and the "only uncovered mummy on exhibition in the world."[30] This enthusiastic bombast lured crowds of locals to the train car, where they paid ten cents to see the show, a quintessential dime museum on rails. There was nothing dignified about these displays, which might pose mummies alongside such attractions as a bearded lady, a giant octopus, or even Abraham Lincoln's last bowel movement.[31]

With so much money to be made from imported mummies, newspapers in the nineteenth and early twentieth centuries reported on the fluctuating prices of ancient cadavers as supplies from Egypt ebbed and flowed.[32] In 1903, the customs office in Philadelphia tried to impose a 20% ad valorem tax on mummies entering the United States, but a protest by mummy importers was upheld.[33] A dispute over import duties on mummies inspired this tongue-in-cheek front-page commentary:

> The thanks of the nation are due the most excellent and most sapient gentlemen who have removed the last obstacle to the free importation of mummies. . . . Lives there a man with soul so narrow and sordid who would rather have free beef and mutton than an untaxed mummy?[34]

One Scottish critic described as "sickening" and "sad" the humiliating spectacle of exhibited mummies: "I question if a single human being is benefited by gazing on the leathern lineaments and limbs of ancient priests or kings."[35] His accusatory finger pointed directly at the United States:

American visitors to Egypt are accounted the best customers of Egyptian body-snatchers. They are glad to return home with a mummy; they are proud of being able to invite their friends to see it unrolled.[36]

He wondered whether Americans would think differently if their own prim cemeteries were someday emptied "in order to discover human remains and bring them to the surface, there to be sold to strangers from beyond the sea in quest of curiosities, or else to be put on exhibition at home?"[37] A similar argument appeared in 1930, addressed to the readers of the *New York Times*.[38] Americans were not alone; the British were bringing home so many mummies from Egypt that the bodies were sometimes listed among the donations dropped off for charity organizations.[39]

A FAIR SHOWING

Most people attending the expositions and world's fairs of the nineteenth and early twentieth centuries expected to see at least one Egyptian mummy among the exhibits. The consummate showman P. T. Barnum knew this well when he published an essay titled "What the Fair Should Be" for those planning the World's Columbian Exposition (Chicago World's Fair) of 1893.[40] Barnum proffered his "million-dollar idea" of renting from Egypt the mummies of Ramses II, the supposed pharaoh of the Exodus, and of the foster-mother of Moses. That scheme faltered, as did another from Alexander Taliaferro offering the sarcophagus and bones of Cleopatra for exhibition, asking only $60,000 to negotiate the deal.[41] This was allegedly the real Cleopatra, unlike the "impostors" reported elsewhere. According to some, her body had been conveyed to Paris by Napoleon and later buried beneath a lilac bush in the gardens of the Bibliothèque nationale.[42] Macabre details about curses and strange worms emerging from her body enlivened this tale, much to the dismay of French authorities who turned away generations of gullible petitioners determined to dig up whatever was left of the queen.[43] A twenty-year investigation determined in 1952 that the grave in the garden was not of a mummy at all, but of someone killed during a Parisian street brawl.[44] Meanwhile, other rumors put the crumbling mummy of the Ptolemaic queen in a glass case curated at the British Museum.[45] Yet another alleged mummy of Cleopatra toured the United States until the venture went broke in Chicago and the mummy was unwrapped only to reveal the skeletal remains of a man.[46] At least one genuine ruler of ancient Egypt did end up in North America, however. The body was taken to Canada by James Walter Douglas Sr. in the nineteenth century and sold to a freak-show collection in Niagara Falls, where its true identity remained unknown.[47] The royal status of the mummy was discovered in 1999 after which the mummy of Ramses I was sent home to Egypt in 2003 from Emory University in Atlanta.[48]

The impulse to exploit mummymania at the 1893 Chicago World's Fair produced only a pale shadow of what Barnum had promoted. Near the entrance, visitors encountered a barker who directed them to an exhibit where a "glib-tongued lecturer" did not bother to admit that the displayed mummies of Ramses and his family were not genuine.[49] Complained one reporter, "With so many poky and spookish objects in the world that are real it is un-called for to go and make fac-similes of mummies, and then charge ten cents to look at them."[50] Clearly, the point of the exhibition was to offer the public something spooky to see, and fake mummies did not merit a visitor's dime. People demanded the real macabre. A few authentic, though not regal Egyptian mummies did adorn the 1893

World's Fair. For example, the German carpet and antiquities dealer Otto Theodor Graf exhibited the well-preserved mummy of a young girl from his collection.[51] Another mummy, dubbed the "Gilded Lady" (now in Chicago's Field Museum), appeared also.[52] A year after acquiring the Gilded Lady from Graf, the Field Museum's president, Edward Ayer, traveled to Egypt, where he purchased about twenty more mummies.[53]

There was no shortage of fairs or mummies to adorn them. In the closing years of the nineteenth century, a widely traveled agricultural equipment dealer named George W. Lininger purchased the contents of an Egyptian tomb, including its mummies. These were exhibited at the Trans-Mississippi International Exposition in 1898, and later donated to the University of Nebraska at Lincoln.[54] At the Louisiana Purchase International Exposition (1904 St. Louis World's Fair), one of the most popular attractions was its display of two mummies, one of them described as the daughter of an ancient nobleman with her face unwrapped so that "visitors may study the actual features of a fellow human being who died more than 2,700 years ago."[55] Crowds also flocked to see the Egyptian mummies exhibited at the Portland, Oregon Exposition in 1905, especially one called "the Rockefeller mummy" because one bystander had remarked to another, "If he don't look like John D. Rockefeller from the nose up I'll eat a chunk out of his coffin."[56] The 1940 New York World's Fair featured a mummy named Harwa in its General Electric exhibit; the corpse famously arrived by airplane, after it had been inadvertently flown to the San Francisco Fair a week earlier.[57] This mummy, when not on tour, was hailed as more popular in Chicago than the White Sox at Comiskey Park.[58]

Often in conjunction with fairs, museums, and other venues, Egyptian mummies developed strong associations with seminaries, colleges, and universities. Campuses, unfortunately, tended to be as unsafe as any other form of makeshift mummy repository. For instance, Yale University acquired its first mummy in 1858, but it was soon lost in an attic for nearly half a century before being rediscovered.[59] Another mummy arrived there in 1909, spinning a fascinating history in the American press. It was awaited in New Haven with great anticipation and wildly rumored to be one of the Ramesside pharaohs, valued at $30,000.[60] Speculation soon slipped down a notch, identifying the body as that of Rha, supposedly pharaoh's unfortunate chief baker who was hanged in the biblical book of Genesis.[61] The fame of this mummy gave license to a long tale in which he fictitiously tours New York on his way to Yale.[62] The busy body fancies himself more upstanding than "Miss Cleo Ptolemy" as he puffs away on a cigarette and makes light of modern life. Our cars, food, subways, and such do not impress the "Nilesian mummy" at all, who concludes: "No, I'm going back into my box to wait until some thing new happens. I saw everything in Egypt, and so far as I can tell, nothing of importance has taken place since." This mummy never did return to the Nile, however, since on the front page of the same edition of the *New York Times* he was announced to be the property of the Yale secret society Skull and Bones.[63] The mummy was intended to be used for initiation rites.[64]

In about 1884, Professor James Van Benschoten smuggled to Wesleyan University a mummy he had purchased; it languished for decades in an attic until retrieved for study in 1978.[65] A few years later, a student stole this mummy and laid it in a classmate's bed, a prank that left across campus an incriminating trail of "skin chips" flaking from the body.[66] In 1885, missionaries purchased a group of mummies for eight dollars each. The mummies were then donated to various institutions such as the College of Wooster in Ohio and Westminster College in Pennsylvania. One of the mummies served in 1886 as the main attraction for the Greenville Citizen's Hose

Company Exhibition and accumulated over the years many names scratched into its coffin by vandals. Another of the missionaries' mummies went to Erskine College in South Carolina, where in 1892 it was consumed in a campus fire.[67]

In 1895, two female mummies were given to the Woman's College of Baltimore, one of which president Goucher partially unwrapped before a gallery of spectators.[68] Hobart College (now Hobart and William Smith Colleges) in 1897 acquired a female mummy of the Ptolemaic period.[69] In 1912, the University of Illinois at Champaign-Urbana displayed an Egyptian mummy head and shroud in its newly opened archaeological museum.[70] Emory University acquired a royal mummy in 1921.[71] The collecting of mummies by institutions of higher learning remains ongoing: Memphis State University paid a Detroit pawn shop $40,000 in 1988 for the mummy of an Egyptian male.[72]

PIECES AND IMPOSTORS

Keeping mummies intact has been a millennial problem. In antiquity, embalmed bodies were sometimes torn apart by robbers in search of hidden valuables. This sad fate befell many mummies in the medieval and modern periods as well, but by then the commodification of Egyptian corpses for medicine, showpieces, and other purposes increased the danger. By the nineteenth century, mummy fragments circulated widely across America. In 1853, a private museum on Broadway in New York included in its cabinets an assortment of mummies and coffins plus four mummified skulls, one footless leg, six hands, and four feet.[73] Some of these appendages were later loaned as props to a traveling Athenaeum lecturer.[74] Mummy heads were quite popular for promoting all sorts of bizarre theories. For example, one supposed "brain expert" used them to demonstrate to the press that "Man's Brain Power Will Always Be Superior to That of Woman's."[75] Similarly, the Philadelphia physician Samuel George Morton's research collection of human skulls included those of a hundred Egyptian mummies, which served as the basis for his controversial work *Crania Aegyptiaca* (1844).[76] Morton was a believer in the radical notions of contemporary phrenologists, pointing out in his tome which skulls he assumed had belonged to lunatics and slaves.[77] Some of the skulls in Morton's collection were borrowed as props for a traveling show mounted by the craniologist George Gliddon, who unrolled mummies as part of his wildly popular lectures.[78] Newspapers reported that Gliddon easily sold three hundred tickets at five dollars each for his performances.[79] Mummies might also be used to denounce unpopular scientific theories that would turn out to be valid. For instance, before the infamous "Monkey Trial" in which he prosecuted schoolteacher John Scopes for promoting the theory of evolution, William Jennings Bryan cited the mummy of King Tut as proof that Darwin was wrong.[80] Bryan invited audiences to observe that Tutankhamun's head looked "no more monkeylike" than people of the twentieth century.

The availability of mummified body parts increased as Egyptomania surged in the late nineteenth and early twentieth centuries.[81] For example, in 1885 the wealthy philanthropist Adolph Sutro exhibited in San Francisco a collection that included the mummified head of an Egyptian female alongside "several perfect hands and feet."[82] An 1895 tea party for the young ladies of Oshkosh, Wisconsin, featured a mummy's hand for all to ponder during a talk on human mortality.[83] In the same year, the hand of a mummy was put on display in the window of E. E. Gallogly's drugstore in Butte, Montana; local papers announced that the relic was the "pretty little paw" of Moses's Egyptian rescuer.[84] Yet another relic was long touted as the very hand of Cleopatra that once held the asp to her breast.[85] The Reverend Dr. Charles Robinson of Harlem, New York, claimed to possess the head of the pharaoh Merneptah, purchased for five dollars in 1898:

> "In all probability you are gazing on the head of the Pharaoh of the Ten Plagues," said Dr. Robinson [to a reporter], "and if so those are the lips from which came the famous question: 'Who is Jehovah that I should obey him?' He probably knows now who He is."[86]

In 1909, a husband and wife from Pennsylvania allegedly owned the head of the great Queen Hatshepsut. Later believing the skull carried a curse that killed her husband and son, the widow in 1915 donated the head to the Carnegie Museum.[87]

Mummy fragments made possible another scourge—the marketable Frankenmummy.[88] As the term suggests, these were mummies cobbled together from bits and pieces, producing a wrapped and ready showpiece from less expensive "spare" parts. Wheresoever the modern mummy market could not meet public demand, enterprising souls worldwide filled the void in this way. They manufactured fake mummies in prodigious numbers that were hawked to traveling shows, dime museums, store-window decorators, and others.[89] Although reliable statistics are impossible to calculate, it is likely that fakes eventually overtook the marketing of authentic mummies. Warned one writer: "It may be thought hardly possible that the makers of spurious antiquities could copy the mummies and their cases. And yet there is no doubt that this has been done."[90] In 1889, a Philadelphia newspaper warned its readers of "Mummy Manufactories" with "hundreds of bogus pharaohs turned out yearly."[91] The story featured a thriving business near the source, at

Luxor, where fresh modern corpses purchased for three shillings were eviscerated, smoked, wrapped, and sold for a hefty profit: "It is no longer necessary to go digging in musty catacombs for Ramses or any of his contemporaries. We can have them made to order . . . kings, queens and princes at very reasonable figures."[92] Actual mummies of humble origins were often "upgraded" to royal status, turning an investment of $20 worth of modest remains and faked adornments into a pharaoh's body that might sell for thousands.[93] In 1929, one such fake stirred a police investigation in New York City when an electrician stumbled upon the "corpse" in a dark cellar said to be haunted.[94]

Dummy-mummy factories operated across Europe and the United States, sometimes without the use of human remains at all. A headline in one California newspaper screamed: "EGYPTIAN MUMMIES MADE WHILE YOU WAIT."[95] The story focused on a local factory that had reportedly produced fifteen to eighteen "Egyptian" mummies every week for twenty-seven years, using a creative framework of wood, plaster, clay, cotton, and parts of a cow. This would amount to more than twenty-one thousand bogus mummies. Newspapers regularly poked fun at the enormous mummy craze and the industry that fed it. One comic showed two travelers aboard an ocean liner, one of them bragging, "I bought the original mummy of King Hokus Pokus!" The other counters, "You're wrong—I bought the original mummy of King Hokus Pokus!" Another cartoon depicted a fashionable traveler informing her Egyptian guide, "I want a mummy of Prince Notatall!" to which the man replies, "Sorry Ma'am—we're out of Prince Notatall mummies, but we'll have a shipment tomorrow."[96]

Some of the most convincing Frankenmummies were of course fashioned from real mummified remains that were cleverly assembled and attractively packaged. In 1928, newspapers reported the embarrassing discovery that the pride of Hackensack, the mummy of an alleged princess, was nothing of the sort: "The prize exhibit of the Bergen County Historical Society for the last 26 years . . . was a dummy" consisting of two mismatched feet, a hand but no wrists, a drilled-out skull, and rag stuffings.[97] The curator incinerated the remains.

DISPOSING OF THE DEAD, AMERICAN STYLE

The fate of all imported mummies hung in a balance more terrifying than the scales tended by the god Anubis. Many ancient bodies ended up burned, abandoned, rebuilt, or even reburied as "saved" Christian souls. A New York antiquarian in 1888 returned home from a trip to find that some children had been given as a plaything his "priceless" mummy hand bearing a ring. The kids tore apart the hand and then sold the ring to a local ragman for ten cents and a stick of candy.[98] In 1902, a proud Texan displayed a withered mummy hand in a glass box at his home in Galveston.[99] Two years later, when the hand began to disintegrate, the owner buried it beneath a banana tree on the island. Another mummy's hand was owned by Texas pioneer John B. Dunn, who amassed a large museum collection composed primarily of weapons.[100] According to the Dunn family, the hand was perhaps a stolen relic sold to their patriarch; it was later given to the Corpus Christi Museum and then passed on to the Witte Museum in San Antonio.[101] A mummified toddler named Amun-Her Khepesh-Ef was purchased for ten dollars in 1886 and displayed briefly before being stored in the attic of the Sheldon Museum in Middlebury, Vermont.[102] After decaying for many years, the mummy was cremated and its ashes buried beneath a tombstone bearing a Christian cross and an Egyptian ankh, just to cover all bases.

Celebrating American holidays sometimes called for the abuse of an Egyptian corpse. In 1887, a mummified "princess" entertained celebrants for Washington's birthday at the New Brunswick Theological Seminary in New Jersey, where she was publicly unrolled.[103] Of course, "unwrapping" or "unrolling" a mummy generally required a violent display of hacking, sawing, and cracking asunder amid clouds of dust. After being dismembered before a rapt audience, pieces were often distributed to guests like party favors.[104] Worse was the public explosion of an Egyptian mummy as a macabre sort of firework for San Francisco's New Year's festivities in January 1876.[105]

Later in the nineteenth century, three Egyptian mummies brought to America by Jeremiah Lynch were donated to San Francisco's Bohemian Club and the Golden Gate Park Museum. Unfortunately, the so-called princess lodged in the Bohemian Club was incinerated during the catastrophic 1906 earthquake, while another of the mummies was crushed by the collapsing walls of the museum.[106] The surviving mummy, along with two others donated in 1901 by M. H. de Young, were joined in 1917 by Irethorrou, a replacement secured by Lynch. All four now rest in the collection of the Fine Arts Museums of San Francisco.[107] In 1916, "a most valuable mummy of the royal family" was bought at auction for twenty-five cents after it was abandoned at a custom house by its American owner.[108] Later, three Egyptian mummies wound up in the unclaimed parcels department of the American Railway Express Company in 1924 after the circus to which they belonged went bust; they were sold to a saloonkeeper in New York's Bowery.[109] In July 1911, the county sheriff was summoned to a Massachusetts hay barn to investigate a suspicious body found inside; the corpse was that of an Egyptian mummy stashed away at the farm.[110]

In 1980, US newspapers carried the story of an Egyptian mummy for sale at a cluttered coin and stamp shop in Michigan; the asking price was $75,000.[111] This may seem an exorbitant price compared to the previous century, but ancient mummies and modern merchandising made a potent combination: consider that a poster for the 1932 Boris Karloff film *The Mummy* sold at auction in 1997 for $453,000.[112] The modern disposition of another mummy stirred international controversy in 1996.[113] The unwrapped body of a "royal princess" had been bought in Egypt during the 1920s.[114] It was first exhibited in a wild animal farm and later sold to a shoe salesman. The mummy changed hands twice more, and in 1992 landed in an antiques store near a sign that read: "Is there life after death? Trespass here and find out." The new owner entertained offers for the corpse, including $30,000 from a Brazilian businessman and a set of Harley-Davidson motorcycles from San Diego's Museum of Death. When the Egyptian government announced a possible claim on the mummy in 1996, the US Customs Service stepped into the dispute. The high-profile Egyptian archaeologist Zahi Hawass told the press, "If this man keeps this mummy, I hope there is a curse on him."[115] The defiant shopkeeper threatened to dump the mummy into Maine's Kennebec River rather than lose money on his investment. In the end, Egyptian authorities lost interest when it was determined that the mummy was that of a male commoner, not a royal princess.[116] Unfazed, Lewis rebranded his prize as a temple priest found by Howard Carter in 1922 during the excavation of King Tut's tomb. In 1985, a family in Memphis, Tennessee, reported a mummy's head inside a hatbox stored in their attic. A relative had carried the relic home from Egypt in the 1850s.[117] A Bronx family in 1991 still kept a prized mummy hand on display in their bedroom.[118]

In 2003, an Egyptian mummy's head rolled out of an old plaid flannel shirt at an estate sale in Cayuga County, New York.[119] The home of mummy expert Bob Brier has topped that with a private collection of body parts including a skull and a left arm whimsically named "Lefty."[120]

Some mummies have become persona non grata in their host museums. The Brooklyn Museum in 1957 owned "an unwrapped and unwanted" Egyptian mummy of "a nice kindly old man" that curators decided to get rid of in one way or another.[121] The first plan was to burn the body, but the devout Christian charged to do so objected on religious grounds. Second and third plans either to bury the corpse or to ship it elsewhere ran afoul of the local board of health, which demanded a physician's certificate attesting the cause of death before burial or removal from the premises. A television station in Chicago offered to accept the mummy for use in its commercials.[122] Eventually dubbed "Melvin the Mummy," the body was carefully rewrapped and put on display in the Brooklyn Museum's Mummy Chamber.[123] A mummy named Tothmea in the Schenectady Museum received a similar reprieve in 1972.[124]

In 1971, the famous Neiman Marcus Christmas catalog offered authentic his and hers empty Egyptian coffins as a luxury gift, unsuspecting until after the sale that a mummy actually resided in one of them.[125] This was not the first marketing scheme to go awry. In 1898, B. J. Johnson & Company introduced Palmolive soap, a bath product containing an "exotic" blend of palm and olive oils (hence the name); marketers used mummies and their coffins to advertise the soap as an ancient Egyptian beauty secret.[126] The more the public saw of real mummies, however, the less they wanted to see one reflected in their mirrors; Palmolive changed its approach. Indeed, during the twentieth century, the reception of Egyptian mummies took a dark turn. They became less like the exotic, even erotic beauties once touted by the press, and increasingly more neurotic and threatening for readers of pulp fiction and the moviegoing public. Mummies had become the monsters of our imaginations.

Chapter 4

Mummies of the Imagination

A voice brittle and incredibly evil came from the puffed blue lips of that horrible face. There it stood—the mummy from the ancient prehistoric past—towering above them—forceful, dynamic, gorged with life!

—Harvey Comics, 1952[1]

FRIGHTENED WHISPERS

As a child, the mummies I met in my comic books were tormentors adrift in time. They were brittle, evil, horrible beings mysteriously potent and gorged with life. In the case cited above, yet another mad professor testing the boundaries between sorcery and science unleashed upon the world a mummy whose eyes "burned with a terrible intensity—and those who caught their gaze—were sucked into a Hell!" The creature's "unearthly mind-power" meant doom for the foolish old archaeologist, but his terrified daughter found rescue in the arms of her resourceful fiancé. The good, the mad, and the ugly all availed themselves of a bewildering mix of spells and secret chemicals.

On the day that I first met Ankh-Hap, he was surrounded by throngs of people corrupted by this legacy of American mummymania. My contemporaries may never have swallowed a dose of granulated mummy to cure a fever, never have invited their neighbors to share in a mummy striptease, and never have shopped for shoes at a store with a mummy propped inside the front window, but they had all seen lots of Egyptian mummies in movies, magazines, cartoons, comic books, toys, and advertising.[2] These were mummies of the imagination, the monstrous offspring of the mistreated corpses that had come to America in the previous century. Actual dead bodies surrendering quietly to public dismemberment, many of them seen primarily as inert objects of medical curiosity, gave way to repulsive ambulatory creatures intent on revenge.[3] The newly imagined mummy mumbled and stumbled about, looking for unsuspecting victims on whom to unleash its occult powers. In the museum, I overheard small children warning each other in nervous whispers not to wake the mummy. They expected the corpse to fulfill its well-known destiny by rousing, strangling a patron or two with its stringy arms, and then escaping into the world. Who could blame them? Had they ever known a mummy to do anything else?

MUMMIES AS MONSTERS

Buried deep in the modern psyche lies a troubled conscience for the despoliation of ancient tombs. Those feelings usually bubble to the surface in one of two ways: either we imagine that the dead do not really mind, and may even enjoy their liberation; or more often, we fashion from our fears a vindictive spirit that inevitably haunts or hurts us. The monsterization of mummies has been a gradual process, worsened in the nineteenth century by writers of Gothic fiction and accelerated in the twentieth by the horror film industry.[4] Seldom today do we encounter the kinds of mummies imagined two centuries ago when they might be beautiful, witty, and festive.[5] For example, Albert Smith's "Mr. Grubbe's Night with Memnon" (1845) gives us the adventure of a dull pedant who finds himself locked inside the British Museum, where all the Egyptian antiquities come to life after dark.[6] The delighted Mr. Grubbe joins the revels and dances with the reanimated mummy of "a fair young daughter of the Nile" with "soft downy cheeks, roguish kissable lips, and supernaturally-sparkling eyes" before being overcome by swirling mummy-dust.[7]

Likewise, an explorer in Théophile Gautier's *The Romance of a Mummy* (1863) falls desperately in love with the beautiful mummy of Queen Tahoser.[8] This mummy is hardly the dismal, deadly, demented creature met in film and literature today. In Grant Allen's "My New Year's Eve Among the Mummies" (1879), the narrator adores the beautiful mummy of an Egyptian princess so much that he tries to have himself embalmed to join her forever.[9] The novel *The Twin Soul, or The Strange Experiences of Mr. Rameses*, published anonymously by Charles Mackay in 1887, features a dazzling reawakened female mummy wooed by competing lovers, one ancient and the other modern.[10] These literary characters are as likely to be tormented by love and lust as by some malicious curse, as in Sir Arthur Conan Doyle's "The Ring of Thoth" (1890) in which a lovely female mummy is stalked across thirty-five centuries by an ancient lovelorn priest.[11] The versatile writer Edgar Allen Poe, who is often credited as the first author of detective fiction, imagines in "Some Words with a Mummy" (1845) an erudite, somewhat comical corpse whimsically named Allamistakeo.[12] The story involves an unswathed mummy awakened by electric shock who then discusses with his guests phrenology, mesmerism, architecture, and other subjects to determine whether ancient or modern was the more advanced civilization.[13]

These mild-mannered, intelligent creatures harbor little malevolence, but hints of a forthcoming hysteria may be found in Jane Webb's *The Mummy! A Tale of the Twenty-Second Century* (1827).[14] This rambling novel, heavily influenced by Mary Shelley's *Frankenstein*, describes the resuscitation of Pharaoh Cheops's mummy by applying galvanic shocks inside his pyramid.[15] The tale introduces a now-standard warning against disturbing a mummy and paints a frightening image of the awakened figure, flexing the full vocabulary of an inchoate genre: *awful, appalling, vindictive, dreaded, ghastly, scornful, demoniac, unearthly, fearful, fiend, horrid, icy, supernatural, withering,* and *withered.* Yet this garrulous mummy turns out to be wise and benevolent in spite of appearances, more misunderstood than monstrous. Less redemptive creatures were eventually uncoffined by writers such as Jane G. Austin, whose story "After Three Thousand Years" (1868) brings to the fore a malevolent female mummy who takes her revenge on the defilers of her tomb by means of an ill-fated scarab necklace.[16] Louisa May Alcott followed in 1869 with a short story titled "Lost in a Pyramid: or, The Mummy's Curse."[17] The secondary title emphasizes the sinister powers of the Egyptian dead, in this case the mummy of a sorceress whose body is burned by a modern explorer to light his way through a pyramid. The angry sorceress eventually wreaks her revenge upon the malefactor and even his innocent bride as well.[18] Another sorceress dominates Henry Rider Haggard's very popular *She: A History of Adventure* (1886), which also depicts the burning of mummies for torchlight.[19] In this instance, the dry bodies were tied to stakes and the hair lit on fire, with flames leaping from the poor wretches' ears and mouths; when the mummy was consumed down to the ankles, the feet were kicked away and another corpse lighted to take its place.

The genre now had in place some of the distinctive features of modern mummy fiction: highly evocative language, a fateful warning against tomb robbery, the ability of vengeful mummies to reanimate, and their persistence in hunting down their victims to punish them directly or by means of an amulet or other object. Literary mummies were evolving. The contrast between the mummies in Conan Doyle's "The Ring of Thoth" (1890) and his short story "Lot No. 249" (1892) is noteworthy.[20] Quite unlike the amiable former, Doyle's reanimated mummy in the latter has all the murderous intent of subsequent monsters, although not yet burdened by a lumbering gait as it pursues its victim:

> As he [Abercrombie Smith] rushed madly and wildly through the night, he could hear a swift, dry patter behind him, and could see, as he threw back a glance, that this horror was bounding like a tiger at his heels, with blazing eyes and one stringy arm out-thrown.[21]

Reanimating these corpses involved all manner of ministrations. Set among the Apis bulls buried at Memphis, Charles Mansford's story "At the Pyramid of the Sacred Bulls" (1896) includes the mummy of a certain Lady Arga, whose remains conceal a pearl sought by a tomb raider who revives her:

> Much as he trembled at the task he set himself to, he took the wax from the mummy's ears, he dissolved the film upon the eyelids, he drew back the tongue till it rested in its right place. Then, as though bringing the drowned to life, he raised and dropped the mummy's arms at regular intervals. . . . The minutes, slowly

moving like hours, monotonously passed on. Then—then— yes!—*the lips of the mummy quivered!*[22]

Deactivating mummies was just as harrowing. In "The Story of Baelbrow" (1898) by E. and H. Heron, even fiction's great detective of the supernatural, Flaxman Low, must struggle with silencing the eviler variety of mummies.[23] The Sherlock-styled Flaxman is summoned to Baelbrow after a previously benign ghost turns murderous. The detective deduces that the ghost has somehow merged with a vampire and a plundered Egyptian mummy in order to attack its victims. No thing of beauty or desire, the mummy rises from its coffin with "a high-nosed, dull-eyed, malignant face, the eye-sockets hollow, and the darkened teeth showing" until it is at last shot in the face repeatedly, burned, and sunk into the sea.[24] Another psychic detective, Dr. John Silence, solves the case of "The Nemesis of Fire" in the works of Algernon Blackwood (1909).[25] The fictional detective relates to his companion: "This case is really typical of all stories of mummy-haunting, and none of them are cases to trifle with . . . for the mummies of important people . . . were very effectively protected, as you have seen, against desecration, and especially against destruction."[26] Of course, he is proved right when the unearthed mummy suddenly "writhed, and, with a faint rustling of the immemorial cerements, rose up, and, through sightless and bandaged eyes, stared across the yellow candle-light at the woman who had violated it."[27] Other psychic detectives, including Seabury Quinn's Jules de Grandin and Sax Rohmer's Moris Klaw, also solved mysteries involving mummies.[28]

Gradually these tales immortalized in chilling words the modern villainization of mummies. Bram Stoker, most famous for his Gothic evocation of Count Dracula, imagines in *The Jewel of Seven Stars* (1903) such horrors about a sinister mummy that he was asked to publish a second version (1912) with a less disturbing ending.[29] Bryson Taylor's *In the Dwellings of the Wilderness* (1904) describes a demonic mummy that attacks the Egyptologist who unearthed it, attaching itself to its victim and sucking his blood: "It came and I felt its arms around my neck ... when I tried to get away, it clung, clung like a leech, with feet and hands and teeth!"[30] Ambrose Pratt's *The Living Mummy* (1910) adds a mad wizard to the widening genre.[31] Writers strove incrementally to elevate our sense of horror by combining vicious mummies with other terrifying creatures such as witches, serpents, cannibals, ghosts, vampires, swarms of flesh-eating beetles, and even giant "tomb-spiders" that feast on the dead and crawl upon the living, as in Robert Spencer Carr's "Spider-Bite" (1926).[32]

The taxed imaginations of fiction writers needed a periodic boost from real-world events. For example, the tragic sinkings of large ships animated many muses. The belief that mummies could destroy oceangoing vessels had a very long history.[33] In fact, many people believed that a single cursed mummy coffin managed to sink the *Titanic* in 1912, the *Empress of Ireland* in 1914, and then the *Lusitania* in 1915.[34] As wild as this assertion turns out to be since the accursed artifact was never actually aboard any of these vessels, an even bolder claim was soon to follow from the Valley of the Kings in Egypt.[35]

THE CURSE

In 1921, a professor of bacteriology warned the American public: "Death and destruction is likely to lurk in the household that has a mummy in the bric-a-brac department. Keep your mummies incased."[36] He feared that, if nothing else, mummies might harbor some hidden contagion able to kill those who opened their coffins. Thus, in a world already awash in tales of terrifying mummies and their creepy curses, the discovery of Pharaoh Tutankhamun's tomb in 1922 created a frenzy of overwrought speculation. The team of English archaeologist Howard Carter found the passageway leading down into Tut's tomb in the Valley of the Kings on November 4.[37] Further explorations began later in the month after the arrival of Carter's wealthy patron, George Edward Stanhope Molyneux Herbert, the fifth Earl of Carnarvon. With appropriate fanfare, the grand opening of the burial chamber occurred on February 16, 1923. Just seven weeks later, Lord Carnarvon was dead. The public was ready for a curse story, and the media and their mediums obliged with the infamous curse of King Tut's Tomb.[38] Marie Corelli, a flamboyant best-selling author of psychic melodramas, passed along to the press her own warning a few days before Carnarvon succumbed to an infected mosquito bite.[39] Her "prediction" caused panic. Within hours of Carnarvon's death in Cairo at the age of fifty-seven, many well-educated but terrified compatriots back in England disposed of their Egyptian mummies and other antiquities to avoid being cursed as well.[40] Fears escalated when Sir Arthur Conan Doyle announced to the American press his own belief that ancient occult forces might lie behind Carnarvon's demise.[41]

The public was predisposed to turn popular fiction into fact. As a result, people began compiling a lengthening list of curse victims, as if every adult alive in 1923 was not fated to die at some point regardless. It has mattered little that simple statistics do not support the curse theory.[42] For example, one sensationalized treatment of the subject characterizes Egyptology as "suicide for the advancement of science" and reports ominously:

When Tutankhamen's tomb was discovered, 10 out of 15 people in Europe were at least fifty-five when they died. But only 10 of the 13 persons involved in the tomb's excavation lived that long.[43]

This means that 67% of Europeans could expect to reach age fifty-five, whereas 77% of the supposed curse victims lived that long. The odds clearly favor the allegedly doomed. Howard Carter, in fact, lived another sixteen years and died at age sixty-four; Dr. Douglas Derry, the anatomist who mutilated Tutankhamun's body, died in 1961 at the age of eighty-seven.[44]

Eventually, the list of Tut's victims included persons with little or no connection to the excavations. Thus, after Carter's secretary Richard Bethell joined the list as so-called casualty number 9 in 1929, his seventy-eight-year-old father, Lord Westbury, was added for good measure, along with eight-year-old Joseph Greer, a lad with no Egyptian contacts whatsoever but unfortunate enough to be run over by Lord Westbury's hearse.[45] Warned one newspaper, "Tut Terror Spreads" with the opening line: "Another link of tragedy has been forged in the chain of an ancient curse."[46] Today's tally includes a doctor killed in a car accident in Los Angeles because, sixteen years earlier, he had allegedly been a member of the Tutankhamen expedition—but he was not.[47] For some, Tutankhamun even caused the outbreak of World War II, killing millions of people because in 1939 the BBC had broadcast on the radio the playing of two trumpets buried with the pharaoh's body.[48] When an actual death was not available, the list expanded to include those who broke a leg, got divorced, fell ill, lost a house in a fire, and so on. In San Francisco, a policeman who stood guard over the golden mask of the pharaoh claimed in a lawsuit filed in 1982 that he had suffered a stroke because of the curse.[49] The strangest stretch to satisfy curse enthusiasts is the claim that, though Howard Carter lived a long life, he was doomed never to find another intact pharaonic tomb.[50] It seems strange to consider it a curse to discover "only" one such tomb.

The story of King Tut's curse grew organically out of earlier mummy fiction and helped sustain that genre for decades to come. In 1922, before the discovery of the tomb, writer Clark Ashton Smith penned in his poem "The Mummy" the interesting lines:

> From out the light of many a mightier day,
> From Pharaonic splendour, Memphian gloom,
> And from the night aeonian of the tomb
> They brought him forth, to meet the modern ray . . .
> He is reborn to mock the might of time.[51]

Tut reborn was a godsend to the Gothic imagination. Beginning in June 1923, the pulp magazine *Weird Tales* asked its subscribers, "Have You Been Reading About King Tut?" followed by the first of a flood of mummy stories, Adam Shirk's "Osiris: The Weird Tale of an Egyptian Mummy."[52] This brief narrative featured a doomed archaeologist who has ignored "the horrors of bats and crawling things" to despoil a tomb and who must therefore pay with his life. Angry, ghoulish mummies became a mainstay of pulp fiction, their numbers suddenly increasing threefold and more after the opening of Tut's tomb (Graph 4.1). In the short story "Imprisoned with the Pharaohs" (1924), ghostwritten by H. P. Lovecraft for showman Harry Houdini, the haunted protagonist vilifies ancient Egypt as "the fountain of all darkness and terror!"[53] He describes mummies as the "perverse products of decadent priestcraft."[54] This theme held sway not only in issue after issue of *Weird Tales*, but in other contemporary periodicals as well: *Ghost Stories, Strange Stories, Terror Tales, Horror Stories, Dime Mystery Magazine, Spicy Mystery Stories, Strange*

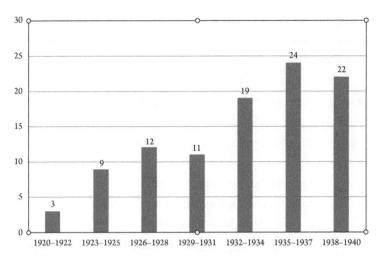

Graph 4.1. Egyptian Mummy Fiction 1920–1940

Tales of Mystery and Terror, and *Fantastic Adventures.* Not until the 1940s did this readership begin to decline appreciably, but by then mummies of the imagination were being supplied in other media besides magazines—most notably, at the movies.[55]

CINEMATIC SENSATIONS

From the silent films of the early twentieth century to the blockbusters of today, mummy movies have a long history anchored solidly in the horror genre. As a result, no published survey of cinematic monsters can be complete without a chapter dedicated to mummies.[56] The embalmed dead of ancient Egypt have been absorbed into the big-screen loony-verse of other terrors ranging from Frankenstein and Dracula to Godzilla, the Wolfman, and the Creature from the Black Lagoon. It was with breathtaking haste that a silent film about the curse of King Tut's tomb appeared within twelve weeks of Lord Carnarvon's death.[57] While a few early filmmakers toyed with comic or romantic treatments, the standard tone and plot for most mummy movies was set in 1932 with the release of Universal's *The Mummy*, portrayed by Boris Karloff (Figure 4.1).[58] Thereafter, a train of movies featured what seemed to be the same archetypical mummy on an endless loop of leg-dragging mayhem.[59] Celluloid mummies were murderous beings adrift in time, hunting their prey in tattered rags with one straining arm outstretched. Whenever mummies were involved, Hollywood's version of history made it clear that archaeologists are idiots. They can

Figure 4.1. Postage stamp commemorating Boris Karloff as the Mummy, 1997
Source: Olga Popova / Shutterstock.com.

easily decipher sinister hieroglyphic warnings but not heed them; they seem incredibly slow to notice their colleagues and other acquaintances dying around them; and when finally alerted to the danger, they apparently can never walk, much less run, just a little faster than a bandaged cadaver. Mummies exemplified hoary old age, even as a potent ingredient in the spell cast by the evil queen in Disney's classic *Snow White and the Seven Dwarfs* (1937): "Mummy dust, to make me old."

As malicious mummies migrated from magazines to movie screens, the relentless constancy of the characters and plots was reinforced by the monotony of the titles: *The Mummy* (1932), *The Mummy's Hand* (1940), *The Mummy's Tomb* (1942), *The Mummy's Ghost* (1944), *The Mummy's Curse* (1944), *The Mummy's Foot* (1949), another *The Mummy* (1959), *The Curse of the Mummy's Tomb* (1964), *The Mummy's Shroud* (1967), *Blood from the Mummy's Tomb* (1971), *The Mummy's Revenge* (1973), *Dawn of the Mummy* (1981), *The Mummy Lives* (1993), *Tale of the Mummy* (1998), *Legend of the Mummy* (1998), another *The Mummy* (1999), *The Mummy Returns* (2001), *The Mummy's Kiss* (2003), *The Mummy Resurrected* (2014), yet again *The Mummy* (2017), *Rage of the Mummy* (2018), *The Mummy Rebirth* (2019), and *Rise of the Mummy* (2021). The garish advertisements for these films guarantee their audiences a terrifying experience. *The Curse of the Mummy's Tomb* (1964) warns its viewers:

> OUT OF AN ANCIENT PHARAOH'S TOMB STALKS A MONSTER OF
> MONSTERS WITH A LUST FOR VENGEANCE AND A THIRST FOR
> TERROR!
> HALF-BONE
> HALF-BANDAGE
> AND ALL BLOOD-CURDLING HORROR!

Monstrous mummies took their toll on those who troubled them, but in time the body count turned. As films became blockbusters with massive CGI budgets, "heroic" mummy-fighters such as Brendan Fraser's character Rick O'Connell began to even the score. It has been calculated that in just three movies, O'Connell somehow dispatched nearly 120 mummies using guns, swords, and dynamite.

Like the convenient elixirs that allegedly brought ancient mummies back to life, television revived many classic mummy movies beginning in the 1950s. Relentless airings kept the public preoccupied with the enduring mythos of violation and revenge. Boris Karloff's mummy was immortalized in a 1963 Aurora plastic model kit bought and built by kids like me who then hid the hideous result deep in our closets. This monster was almost as frightening as the 1966 Japanese TV version equipped with laser-firing eyes.[60] Revived mummies made appearances in many episodes of popular television series, including *Jonny Quest* (1964), *Spider-Woman* (1979), *Hart to Hart* (1981), *Tales from the Darkside* (1987), *Tales from the Crypt* (1990), *Quantum Leap* (1992), *Goosebumps* (1995), and *Doctor Who* (2014). The children's animated series *Mummies Alive!* (1997–1998) featured various Egyptian corpses battling in the modern world. Later, twenty-six episodes of an animated series for children based on the 1999 film *The Mummy* aired on television from 2001 to 2003.

These films and TV shows scared generations of us to death (or rather, about death) with their tales of curses and ruthless corpses. At the same time, celluloid and earlier tabloid mummies embodied the contested political and social currents of the day in matters of cultural appropriation, colonialism, racism, Orientalism, and commercial exploitation.[61] In the tense darkness of a hushed theater or private living room, we occasionally gasped aloud and understood why these angry mummies kept coming after us time after time. A collective guilt lay behind these tales, reminding viewers and readers of their complicity in the ravaging of Egypt. Muddling science, superstition, and the occasional séance, storylines questioned the sanity of Westerners who thought too much of themselves and too little of the exoticized cultures they were plundering by right of conquest. Fictional archaeologists with their sense of racial and cultural superiority were forced to confront their own limitations in the light—or darkness—of a lost Egyptian lore that defied rational explanation. With growing unease, we witnessed the bodies of ancient Egyptians being bought and sold like slaves and prostituted to covetous collectors; many ancient "princesses" were unwrapped in eroticized gatherings that approximated a gang rape. Disquieting questions of ethics and morality led some filmmakers to lighten the mood with occasional comic treatments, such as Universal's *Abbott and Costello Meet the Mummy* (1955) and the bizarre movie *Bubba Ho-Tep* (2003), but this did not help.

Children have been no less conflicted than their parents, especially youngsters growing up since the seventies with mummies imagined as both cute cartoon characters and fiendish animated monsters (Figure 4.2). The former, of course, vanish like wisps whenever kids come face to face with the real thing. In the HMNS lobby, children clearly associated Ankh-Hap with TV's terrifying Mumm-Ra of *Thundercats* (1985–1989) rather than the harmless little mummy appearing in the *Groovie Goolies* animated series (1970–1971). In any case, the key thing they had all read, seen, and heard was that mummies do come back to life. No amount of countervailing mummy humor mattered in that moment—not the silly playground jokes about mummies wrapped up in their work, not the adorable Halloween costumes worn the night before, not the Munchy Mummies Candy in their trick-or-treat bags. Mummies were monsters. Coming soon was a breakfast cereal to remind them called Fruity Yummy Mummy, the latest of General Mills' monster

Figure 4.2. The marketing of mummy monsters for children

cereals that included Franken Berry, Count Chocula, Boo Berry, and Fruit Brute. The gang of movie monsters that once spooked their parents were turned into cartoonish spokes-creatures for sweetened breakfast fare, but all were monsters, nonetheless. As such, the Yummy Mummy was a creation completely and deliberately devoid of historical context. In fact, commercials for this new cereal depicted Franken Berry and Count Chocula discovering their "Egyptian" counterpart inside, of all things, a Mayan pyramid.

Toys and games, too, reflect the modern-day monsterization of mummies. For every hilarious windup plastic mummy Monster Pooper that defecates candy treats as it lurches along, there are dozens of humorless, scary items awaiting children on store shelves. Parents buy them Mummy's Curse glow-in-the-dark plastic cadavers that spring from their coffins while launching rubber bats, spiders, and cobras into the air. Marketers sell zombie mummy playsets, creepy Mummies Alive! action figures, mummified Teenage Mutant Ninja Turtles, plus Lego's Curse of the Pharaohs mummies and the Monster Fighters who attack a mummy from a helicopter. The Matchbox Haunted Mummy's Gold Adventure Set features an evil talking mummy with glowing eyes who grabs passing vehicles and threatens them with a curse. Kids are rewarded for stealing the mummy's treasure.

Playmobil offers four-year-old children an Egyptian Tomb Play Box boldly labeled "HISTORY" filled with jewels guarded by snakes, scorpions, spiders, and a mummy wielding an ax and sword; the grave-robbing "archaeologist" brandishes a handgun. Meantime, an Imaginext toy punishes a trapped treasure hunter by transforming him into a disgusting-looking Egyptian mummy. Morbid Enterprises sells a life-size Deluxe Scary Animated Baby Mummy doll that talks and flails its arms. One popular toy manufactured for children as young as five boasts on the box: "Mummy's arm reaches from the tomb!"[62] In Milton Bradley's vintage board game Voice of the Mummy for ages seven to fourteen, explorers collect a mummy's jewels while responding to commands spoken by the monster using an actual record player hidden beneath his sarcophagus. Video games exploit menacing mummies in many forms, including *Darkstalkers'* Anakaris, a muscled rather than emaciated creature whose bandages can be weaponized. An interactive experience awaits thrill seekers on the Revenge of the Mummy ride at Universal Studios Florida.

HEROES AND HORRORS

In the twentieth century, as mummies joined the ranks of other cinematic monsters in popular culture alongside earlier iterations in pulp magazines, a wave of superheroes began to battle regenerated mummies and their minions. In 1943, for example, Superman was called upon in Paramount's animated short *The Mummy Strikes* to defeat the deadly curse of King Tush. Soon, what pulp magazines had supplied to one generation was passed on via comic books to the next.[63] Beginning in comic books of the 1940s, mummies became the nemeses of Captain America, the Green Hornet, the Thing, Batman, Spiderman, Wonder Woman, The Flash, Blackhawk, and other superheroes.[64] The Marvel Universe created N'Kantu the Living Mummy, a tragic immortal with awesome superpowers, while Dell Comics equipped its murderous Ahmed the Mummy with more of those laser-shooting eyes. Often with half-clad, wholly terrified women on the covers, popular comics such as *Tales from the Tomb, Supernatural Thrillers, Baffling Mysteries, Terror Tales, Nightmare, Eerie, Mister Mystery, Forbidden Worlds, Web of Mystery, Web of Evil,* and *Chamber of Chills* drew demonic mummies engaged in spine-tingling cruelty. They, like their victims, frequently uttered a limited vocabulary laden with vowels: AIEEEE! EEYOW! AAARGH! and AHHHEEEEIIIIOOOOO! An articulate few made dramatic, threatening speeches such as this:

> You ignored the warning I had inscribed on my tomb, therefore, you must die! Greedy, avaricious, beast that you are! Prying into the mystic secrets of the past! Trying to obtain fame and fortune from the sacred relics of the golden age! And now you pay for your greed with your life! Thus the fingers of death close about your throat and send you into the voids of eternity![65]

Today, Zenescope's scantily costumed comic book character Liesel Van Helsing is a monster-hunting hero, often victorious over vampires, but her "greatest challenge" yet is defeating the Egyptian mummy of Amun-Ra.[66]

Children absorb this chilling message very early: *Do not mess with mummies; they are ill-tempered and no end of trouble.* They walk, stalk, mangle, and strangle in a nightmarish world of the deadly undead. As adults, of course, we are expected to outgrow our fears about vampires, werewolves, and ghosts, though perhaps not of mummies. The latter, after all, undeniably exist, a lesson parodied on the TV sitcom *The Office* when an employee declares, "I'm only scared of real things like serial killers or kidnappers, not things that don't exist like ghosts or mummies."[67] When informed that mummies exist in museums around the world, the character is thoroughly horrified by the news. He would not have been happy to meet Ankh-Hap inside the lobby of a modern museum.

Guilt has long resided in the house of horror. Every mummy, real or imagined, comes from a desecrated tomb. Every story about mummies adrift in our modern world begins with a criminal offense. Thus, defilers and destroyers of the dead have deserved little pity, least of all when duly warned. Made-up inscriptions, papyrus admonitions, the forebodings of mediums, curse stories in newspapers, and even the cautionary tales of movies and magazines all served like the exculpatory rattle of a rattlesnake to advise, "Leave me alone or accept your inevitable punishments."[68] There is something about a warning that wakes the dread in all of us, that drowns out our cries of innocence. In the context of mummy lore from the nineteenth and twentieth centuries, did the person who sent Ankh-Hap from Egypt to Texas ever worry about the consequences? I was eventually to find the answer.

Chapter 5

The Mummy-Pits of Egypt

Mummies (human and animal) and Coffins from the Mummy-Pits
of Egypt . . . continually replenished, as sales occur.
                    —Advertisement in *Ward's Scientific Catalogue*, 1891[1]

THE NEW WORLD

The world in which Ankh-Hap was buried bore little resemblance to
the one through which he traveled in the nineteenth and twentieth
centuries. His contemporaries from the last centuries BCE might
now be anywhere and anything from a storefront novelty in Idaho
to a dab of paint on a Renaissance canvas. His mother Maat-Djehuty
may have been ground into a bottle of medicine or his father burned
to cinders in a holiday bonfire. Had he any brothers or sisters, aunts
or uncles, they too must struggle to survive the dangers of modern
Egyptomania. Bizarre stories were being imagined about the dead
of Egypt by people beginning to worry that mummies might be ambulatory, vengeful, and cruel. Ankh-Hap himself (or what remained
of him) was likely to be feared by children convinced that he was an
awakened monster.

Who, I wondered, had brought Ankh-Hap into this new world?
What did they intend to do with his body and coffin? Such mysteries

pose a special challenge for the modern detective. As Sherlock Holmes explains in *The Adventure of the Copper Beeches* (1892), proper detection depends upon three essentials: "Data! Data! Data!" But where was I to find any in a case as cold as this one? The answer lay waiting in another of Holmes's famous aphorisms: "You know my method. It is founded upon the observation of trifles."[2]

TRAVEL DOCUMENTS

An important clue about Ankh-Hap's journey lay concealed in his coffin like a passport left in a traveler's luggage. The HMRP had found some old scraps of paper stuffed around the mummy, wedged there undisturbed as makeshift packing for most of a century. While this tattered and inconspicuous little dossier offered some hope of answering several key questions about Ankh-Hap's travels in America, it would take me another thirty years to piece that puzzle together.

The trifles discovered in the coffin were these:

A. An American Express mailing label attached to brown wrapping paper, addressed to George L. English of Ward's Scientific Establishment, Rochester, New York, from W. L. Bachtell, Milford, Utah, dated May 12, 1914

B. A piece of paper on which was written "Mr. H. O. Frank" in the same handwriting as the label above

C. Newspaper pages from the *Rochester Herald* dated March 25, 1914

D. Newspaper pages from the *Rochester Herald* dated April 1914

E. Newspaper pages from the *Los Angeles Examiner* dated May 10, 1914

F. Newspaper pages from the *Rochester Herald* dated May 29, 1914

These documents were remarkably uniform in origin, quite unlike the scatter of debris sometimes collected in other Egyptian coffins. For example, within the coffin of a mummy housed in a Belgrade museum curators once found candy wrappers, ticket stubs, coins dated between 1953 and 1972, a cigarette butt, and other litter.[3] Inside the coffin of Ankh-Hap, however, the extraneous materials all date to a nine-week span between March 25 and May 29, 1914. Most of the scraps came from Rochester, with a connection there to a company founded in 1862 called Ward's Scientific Establishment. What was the possible link between this business and the HMNS mummy?

Answering these questions was essential in order to establish the complete cultural biography of the mummy and coffin. The first attempts to do so were only marginally successful. As it happened, the company in Rochester was still in operation as Ward's Science, and its obliging president, Henry (Hank) Barbeau, was able to provide some information about George English and his connection to the business.[4] English had exhibited a prize-winning collection of gems and minerals at the 1893 World's Columbian Exposition in Chicago and, in 1905, sold his mineralogical stock to Ward's Natural Science Establishment. In 1913, English became manager of the Mineral Department at Ward's, after which he served as a consulting geologist and mineralogist from 1922 until his retirement in 1934; he died in Rochester on January 2, 1944.[5] Hank Barbeau had no knowledge of Ward's ever handling mummies, nor was he able to help with the names Bachtell and Frank from the coffin dossier.

During my research, I discovered an earlier connection between Bachtell and English, buried in a 1904 science article referencing some crystals removed from a cave in Kansas; at that time English still owned his own minerals company.[6] Since English later worked in the Mineral Department at Ward's, the 1914 mailing label found with the mummy had probably been attached to a packet of mineralogical specimens sent by Bachtell to English. I discovered newspaper accounts that placed Bachtell in the employ of Ward's also; he operated as the company's representative in the American West as late as 1915.[7] Thus, the mailing label fits neatly into the chronology of the other documents in the coffin and with the associations of persons working for, or at least with, Ward's Scientific Establishment. No direct connection between Ward's and Egyptian mummies could be established, however, beyond the presence of these papers in the coffin. We next contacted Karl Kabelac at the University of Rochester, where some of the company's archives were maintained, particularly the papers of its founder, Henry Augustus Ward. This led to a little more information about George English, but nothing relating to Egyptian mummies.[8] The coffin papers presented an unresolved mystery that gnawed at me for years. I had to confess in a 1988 newspaper interview: "The trail . . . is pretty cold."[9]

Fortunately, subsequent decades brought forth expansive new opportunities for archival sleuthing. The painstakingly digitized holdings of many libraries and special collections became increasingly accessible through the internet. In 2017, I filed an online request regarding the Ward's Scientific Establishment archives in Rochester, where documents and letters were being digitized. I was especially grateful to receive an enthusiastic response from Melissa Mead, the John M. and Barbara Keil University Archivist and Rochester Collections Librarian in the Department of Rare Books and Special Collections of the Rush Rhees Library at the University of Rochester. She was not aware of any connection between Ward's and mummies, but she was intrigued by the possibility and eager to assist. In turn, I volunteered to help transcribe documents housed in the collection and pieced from them a story I never expected to find. Letters, diaries, and other documents proved without a doubt that Henry Ward and his company had a long history of gathering and selling mummies and coffins.

Henry Augustus Ward (1834–1906) was a tireless traveler and a collector of everything from minerals and meteorites to mollusks and mastodons (Figure 5.1). He prospected among the lawless mining camps of the American West, where he faced down a gang of stagecoach robbers and accidentally decapitated a miscreant he was helping to hang.[10] He was the sometime companion of famous

Figure 5.1. Henry Augustus Ward
Courtesy of Melissa Mead.

showmen such as "Buffalo Bill" Cody and P. T. Barnum. As a young man with scientific aspirations, he worked with the Swiss-born geologist and zoologist Louis Agassiz at Harvard.[11] Eventually, Ward taught natural history at the University of Rochester while founding a business that made him "the king of museum builders" in America.[12] His clients constituted a who's who of the nation's leading colleges, universities, seminaries, museums, and private collections. In January 1890, he compiled a list of eighty colleges, universities, and other institutions to which he had sold miscellaneous collections costing $1,000 or more each.[13] He zealously exhibited the wonders of natural history in world's fairs and other expositions, such as those in Chicago (1875, 1893), Philadelphia (1876), Allegheny City (1879), Louisville (1880, 1886), Melbourne (1881), Milwaukee (1883), and New Orleans (1884).[14] The foundation for Chicago's renowned Field Museum was laid when Marshall Field purchased for $100,000 the entire display of artifacts from Ward's Natural Science Establishment at the 1893 world's fair.[15] Ward's company trained and employed some of the nation's finest taxidermists, artisans able to complete some very high-profile commissions. For example, in 1885 when the beloved elephant Jumbo was hit head-on and killed by a speeding locomotive, P. T. Barnum hired Ward and his staff to stuff and mount the giant carcass.[16] This enormous task made celebrities of Ward and his workers.[17] Ever the entrepreneur, Ward sold souvenir slivers of Jumbo's shattered tusks and advertised for sale the elephant's enormous heart; the organ weighed forty-six pounds and was eventually sold at a price of $40.[18]

Yet, for all his prominence as a businessman and collector, Ward's active role in the merchandizing of mummies to buyers in nineteenth- and early twentieth-century America has long been hidden from history.[19] His enthusiasm for mummy collecting began early. In 1855 at the age of twenty-one, Ward first ventured into the so-called mummy-pits of Egypt.[20] He traveled in the company of Charlie Wadsworth, an ailing friend whose wealthy father was willing to pay their expenses to tour Egypt and Palestine.[21] Both young men were students of geology and avid collectors of natural history specimens ranging from rocks to animal pelts. On this Nile journey, Ward wrote to his sister Elizabeth pointedly: "I shall try hard for a mummy."[22] By this time, mummies had begun trickling into America, prizes to be stripped in parlors, displayed in store windows, or stacked in museums. They conveyed to admiring gawkers the exotic "otherness" of ancient Egypt. What young student of natural history would not want one?

Ward's efforts swept him up and down the Nile valley by boat, horse, donkey, and foot. Ward's Line-a-Day diary records visits to "the mummy crocodile pits near Osioot [Asyut]" on January 18, the Theban "tombs and mummy-pits with a [touring] party" on March 15, and the "mummy-pits of Manfaloot" on March 23.[23] Ward knew the risks of entering these catacombs. Years earlier, Giovanni Battista Belzoni, the circus strongman who became a renowned explorer and excavator in Egypt, described these pits as dark, dirty, and dangerous. He confessed horror at the sensations they stirred in him, particularly when choking on the dust of decaying corpses:

> Though, fortunately, I am destitute of the sense of smelling, I could taste that the mummies were rather unpleasant to swallow. . . . I sunk altogether among the broken mummies, with a crash of bones, rags, and wooden cases, which raised such a dust as kept me motionless for a quarter of an hour, waiting till it subsided again. I could not remove from the place, however, without increasing it, and every step I took I crushed a mummy in some part or other.[24]

In spite of these discomforts, locals and tourists plundered the mummy-pits relentlessly for souvenirs and medicinal *mumia*. Travelers often embellished their tales of despoliation with all the Gothic terrors expected of such an experience.[25] When the roving Englishman Thomas Legh, a fellow of the Royal Society, visited the mummy-pits at Thebes and Manfaloot in 1813, he described the first of these as follows:

> Our curiosity induced us, during our stay here, to descend into one of the mummy pits that abound in this neighbourhood, but it would be difficult to convey an adequate idea of the disgusting scene of horror we had to encounter. The entrance was through a very narrow hole, nearly filled up with rubbish, by which we made our way into a small room about fifteen feet long and six wide: beyond we reached a chamber somewhat larger. . . . The whole of this chamber was strewed with pieces of cloth, legs, arms, and heads of mummies, left in this condition by the Arabs who visit these places for the purpose of rifling the bodies and carrying off the bituminous substances [*mumia*] with which they have been embalmed. From the chamber above described, two passages lead into the interior and lower part of the mountain, and we penetrated about the distance of a hundred yards into that which appeared the longest. Slipping and crawling amongst the various fragments of these mutilated bodies, we were only able to save ourselves from falling by catching hold of the leg, arm, or skull of a mummy, some of which were lying on the ground, but many still standing in the niches where they had been originally placed.[26]

Legh next visited the region around Asyut, where two of his guides suddenly collapsed and died inside the fetid bowels of the mummy-pits at Manfaloot.[27] Accused of murder for abandoning his guides to their fate, Legh and his companions barely escaped the vengeance of local villagers. The incident was widely reported and long remembered among travelers to Egypt.

One of those familiar with Legh's story was Henry Ward. In a rambling letter to his mentor, Dr. Chester Dewey, Ward described his foray into these same mummy-pits of Manfaloot:

> Leaving part of my escort at the outside, I descended at once with two guides, one of my sailors, & my dragoman, each having a lighted candle in our hand. For the first half-hour the cavern consisted of long horizontal gal(l)eries, connected by low narrow passages, through some of which we crawled with extreme diffi-culty. From the roof hung many thick short stalactites, among which nestled thousands of bats, which flew back & forth past us, threatening constantly to extinguish our lights. Soon how-ever the character of the whole changed, the roof was often too high to be seen, the passages led off in all directions, & opened by little portals into each other, & the whole was one vast lab-yrinth of rooms & halls, pillars & arches, ascents & descents. I hesitated some in trusting myself in a place where to be lost would be almost certain death, but my guides proceeded with such unhesitating directness that I gained confidence to follow. But the real danger lay in the foul & mephitic vapours, which in this very place caused the death of two of Mr. Legh's guides in 1832 [sic],[28] & has permitted few travellers to enter since. I found this only unpleasant at first, for I had been pretty well schooled in this respect at the mummy-pits of Thebes [eight days earlier], but, when I had reached this more inner point, the powerful combination of odours was nearly insupportable. The presence of Ammonia was so great as even to be quite painful to the eyes,

and our lights burned with but half their former clearness. The rocks too were slippery with a carbonaceous deposit, probably from the vapors laden with decomposed animal matter, & everything wore a fuliginous aspect as if it had been the seat of some extensive conflagration. . . .[29] I passed on, desirous of following the fissure to its further extremity. This design however I abandoned after having walked, crept, & crawled for nearly half an hour, for the fissure seemed to grow no narrower, although it was often nearly choked up with stalactites, which reached from the roof to the bodies beneath. Returning, I found that my workmen had cleared a large space, & laid bare the mummied crocodiles, which, with an occasional human body, extended tier below tier, down to an unknown depth.[30]

Ward sent a similar account to his mother in a letter that was shared among family members and friends. In response, Uncle Levi Ward wrote to Henry:

> We all read your journal sent to your mother, through your aunt Susan with much interest. That mummy pit must have been a queer place after all.[31]

Did the young traveler ever acquire his human mummy? Ward mentioned no mummy to his sister when writing home from Thebes in February 1855, but he reported some success to his aunt Elizabeth in April.[32] He informed her that he and Charlie Wadsworth had each filled a barrel and a box with specimens of many types, adding:

> Mine contains a number of antiquities. Mummied heads, hands & feet, (some of the hands with gold rings still on the fingers) mummied crocodiles, & Ibis, Images, Scarabei, &c.

Ward's acquisitions were not uncommon among travelers at the time. Less adventurous visitors stayed out of the pits, choosing—or relenting—to buy the offerings of local vendors "loaded with their ghastly merchandize, some carrying a swathed leg and foot over one arm, others offering a basket full of hands, black and dried up, but the nails perfect and deeply tinted with red."[33] Sixty years later, tourists at Luxor still complained: "Can you imagine anything more disquieting to the nerves, when you are resting and getting ready for luncheon, than to have a villainous child of the desert rush up and lay a petrified human head in your lap and beg you to make an offer?"[34] This "outraged" traveler nevertheless purchased several human extremities to employ as paperweights. Confessed another:

> You can purchase hand, foot, head or any part you want. I have two mummy heads, and bones of various parts of the anatomy.[35]

BRINGING BODIES HOME

Ward knew that his grisly tourist-trove was illegal. He confessed in his letter to Elizabeth: "These [artifacts] are contraband . . . but the banker at Alexandria passes them for me." It is hardly acceptable to say that "everyone else was doing this, too" as a defense of Henry Ward's actions, but at the same time we must acknowledge how different Egypt was then. In the wake of Napoleon's invasion, the country had become "the Wild West of the antiquities trade."[36] Everything from massive obelisks to miniature amulets escaped, often with official sanction, to admirers in Europe and America. Western dignitaries and tourists helped themselves as an entitlement of colonialism, abetted by authorities in Egypt who gave away or sold treasures from the Egyptian Museum itself. All this would irrevocably change when an awakened nationalism in Egypt later asserted its rightful control over its antiquities following the discovery of Tutankhamun's tomb, but by then Henry Ward was long dead. In his lifetime, even archaeologists indulged in the lucrative antiquities trade. The well-intentioned laws against looting imposed by Abbas Pasha I and his successor, Sa'id Pasha, had little real effect. When the latter established Egypt's Service des Antiquités in 1858, he appointed the Frenchman Auguste Mariette as its all-powerful director. The responsibility for protecting Egypt's cultural heritage was placed in the same hands that had illegally plundered the Serapeum and its Apis bulls.[37] In that sort of world, it was relatively easy for Ward to mail home his collection, weighing more than eight hundred pounds, by relying upon his banking agent in Alexandria.[38] His diary reveals that, three days before posting this letter, he had busied himself in Cairo packing his specimens for shipment to America via the port at Alexandria.[39]

Ward was certainly not alone. As reported by the well-known novelist and travel writer Amelia Edwards in *Harper's New Monthly Magazine*:

> A foreign agent and wine-merchant of Cairo assured me, when I returned from the Second Cataract in 1874, that he had that very season already "passed" and shipped no less than eighteen Theban mummies, and many other agents were most likely equally busy and equally successful.[40]

She added that it was no trouble stowing away a royal mummy inside a crocodile or wrapped in a folded tent to be "slipped through the Alexandria custom-house by one of these gentlemen."[41] An American doctor simply stuffed the mummy of a child into his valise and hauled it home to Baltimore.[42] Qualms over such behavior were easily quashed. In the nineteenth century, even someone as sensitive as Amelia Edwards to the cultural legacy of Egypt could excuse the despoliation of antiquities. In 1890, she commented in her immensely popular travelogue *A Thousand Miles Up the Nile*:

> We soon became quite hardened to such sights [violated graves], and learned to rummage among dusty sepulchres with no more compunction than would have befitted a gang of professional body-snatchers. These are experiences upon which one looks back afterwards with wonder, and something like remorse; but so infectious is the universal callousness, and so overmastering is the passion for relic-hunting, that I do not doubt we should again do the same things under the same circumstances. Most Egyptian travellers, if questioned, would have to make a similar confession.[43]

Henry Ward proved her point when he returned to the mummy-pits some years later as a businessman rather than student.

After his 1855 trip to Egypt, Henry Ward continued his studies in natural history while joining the faculty at the University of Rochester in upstate New York. He employed his personal collection of forty thousand fossils and other materials to support his lectures, building for these specimens two structures near campus that he named Cosmos Hall and Chronos Hall (Figure 5.2). On the evening of October 9, 1869, an errant candle ignited a massive blaze in Cosmos Hall; the fire quickly spread to adjacent Chronos Hall as a nearby pond was pumped dry in a losing battle to fight the flames.[44] No one was killed, but one human body lay inside the smoldering wreckage. According to an inventory dated just five weeks earlier by Professor Ward, Cosmos Hall housed his extensive collection of

Figure 5.2. Ward's Cosmos Hall and Chronos Hall, Rochester, NY
Courtesy of Melissa Mead.

natural history specimens that included an "Ethnological Cabinet comprising an Egyptian Mummy and about 100 other Egyptian Antiquities."[45] It cannot be certain whether Ward had acquired this mummy during his explorations in 1855, or some time afterward. The latter seems likely since he mentioned no whole mummy in his letters home from Egypt, unless of course Ward—already an expert in taxidermy and mounted specimens—had pieced this one together from the human remains he had shipped home. Could this have been Ankh-Hap, since his coffin shows clear evidence of considerable smoke and water damage? Certainty is elusive, but Ward did manage to salvage about a quarter of the materials stored in these burned buildings.[46] On the day after the disaster, he recorded laconically in his diary: "Worked all day among ruins of my cabinet buildings."[47] In his monthly journal for October, Ward added: "My private cabinet buildings . . . burned on the eve of the 9th and my entire month was taken up with work connected with the loss."[48] Newspapers reported that damage to Ward's zoological cabinets was less severe than to his mineralogical collection.[49]

The 1869 Rochester fire marked a turning point in Henry Ward's eventful life. Raking the ashes, he decided to give up his teaching career at the university in order to devote all his time and talents to the business venture he called Ward's Natural Science Establishment.[50] He resolved to rebuild his collections, gathering new specimens to stock an emporium filled with marketable fossils, minerals, stuffed animals, skeletal displays, and antiquities. To that end, Henry Ward resumed his travels and returned to the mummy-pits of Egypt in 1877, no longer a student collector on holiday but now a renowned naturalist and savvy businessman. His companion on this excursion was William Hornaday, an American zoologist who later served as the controversial director of the Bronx Zoo.[51] Hornaday described Ward as a genius "composed of raw-hide, whale-bone and asbestos" and founder of "the greatest scientific emporium in the world."[52]

Ward set his sights on Egypt's mummies as one source of revenue for his company. His diary entry for January 23, 1877, reads: "AM to crocodile mummy pits. Day there collecting specimens." Ward also traveled at times with Elbert Eli Farman, the US consul general at Cairo who secured for America the obelisk that now stands in New York's Central Park.[53] Farman published the narrative of a day spent in the mummy-pits at Manfaloot with "Professor Ward, the naturalist of Rochester, N.Y." whose "object was to obtain specimens for the large collections he was furnishing to museums and other institutions."[54]

Even at this late date, Egypt's mummy-pits seemed inexhaustible and remained only partly explored in spite of a ceaseless train of bodies and body parts taken from them.[55] In a sentence stretching almost as long as the mummy trade itself, one writer explained:

> Notwithstanding the depredations that have been committed, the mummies that have been taken away and scattered all over the world, those that have been burnt, and others that now remain in fragments around the tombs, the numbers yet undisturbed, are no doubt infinitely greater; for the practice of embalming is known to have existed from the earliest period recorded in the history of Egypt; and by a rough computation, founded upon the age, the population of the city, and the average duration of human life, it is supposed that there are from 8,000,000 to 10,000,000 of mummied bodies in the vast necropolis of Thebes.[56]

Little wonder that a plunderer who raided the pits at Manfaloot a year or so after Ward's second visit described packing his haul of mummies on donkeys while one of his guides "made a bundle of mummy legs and arms, threw them over his shoulders, and marched on ahead."[57] Sadly, renowned archaeologists often treated the mummies no better. In the diary of Egyptologist William Flinders Petrie, we read:

> The amount of mummification of my premises is embarrassing; all along the way to my tent the place is so strewn with headless mummies, (for I take the heads of all the portrait mummies that are not kept) that what with them, & boxes, & spare wood, I can hardly get in & out. Omar sits on a couple of mummies stowed one on the other for a bench & plays at counters with the gilt buttons from mummy wrappings, on the top of a coffin.[58]

Ward found both crocodile and human mummies at Manfaloot. According to Farman, the larger specimens "could not be taken out through the small, tortuous passage and consequently were undone, broken up and taken out in fragments."[59] It was a common practice for guides to carry daggers so that the mummies could be cut up and carried out in pieces.[60] Farman speculated that the mummies had originally been brought into the caverns through a larger entrance yet undiscovered. When the consul general traveled on, the former professor remained behind at the pits to pack up his mummies. Hornaday would later write in a book about this trip that from Manfaloot they shipped "two mummied crocodiles, a skull, and an armful of mummied arms, legs, and heads of ancient Egyptians."[61] He added that General Stone, chief of staff for the khedive (viceroy of Egypt), had obtained permission for Ward to export two mummies and their coffins.[62] In an article about Ward, Hornaday relates that in February 1877, Ward shipped to America "a large collection of assorted mummies and other antiquities."[63] Ward himself wrote in a letter to the philanthropist Lewis Brooks: "From Egypt I shipped 8 boxes and shall doubtless send a dozen more."[64]

MUMMY INVENTORIES

Archivist Melissa Mead helped me discover handwritten inventories of these Egyptian materials that chronicle Ward's role as an American mummy merchant (Figure 5.3).[65] Listed in a large old ledger are his inventories for each New Year's Day, arranged by country or culture of origin, for example American, Danish, Nubian, Saxon, and so on. The inventory for January 1, 1878, reflects at least some of the Egyptian stock shipped to Rochester the previous February.[66] In addition to bronze artworks, stone sculptures, coins, scarabs,

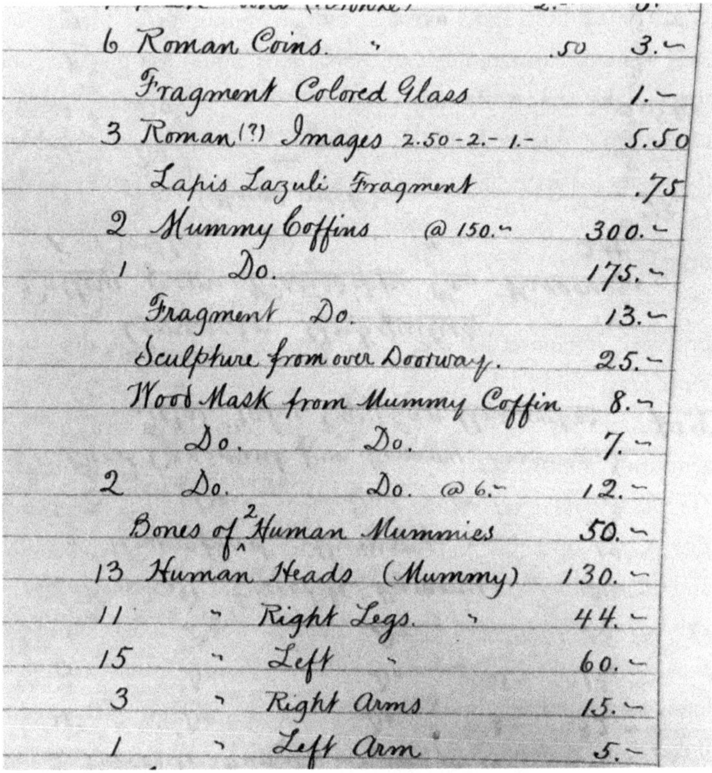

6	Roman Coins. "	.50	3.—
	Fragment Colored Glass		1.—
3	Roman(?) Images 2.50-2.-1.-		5.50
	Lapis Lazuli Fragment		.75
2	Mummy Coffins	@ 150.—	300.—
1	Do.		175.—
	Fragment Do.		13.—
	Sculpture from over Doorway.		25.—
	Wood Mask from Mummy Coffin		8.—
	Do. Do.		7.—
2	Do. Do.	@ 6.—	12.—
	Bones of 2 Human Mummies		50.—
13	Human Heads (Mummy)		130.—
11	" Right Legs. "		44.—
15	" Left "		60.—
3	" Right Arms		15.—
1	" Left Arm		5.—

Figure 5.3. Ward's inventory of Egyptian antiquities, 1879
Courtesy of Melissa Mead.

and other Egyptian antiquities, the inventories discloses in flowing script the following samples of his merchandise:

2 Mummy Coffins	$150.—	300.—
Portion of a Ditto		13.—
Wooden Mask from Mummy Coffin		8.—
" " " " "		7.—
3 " " " " "	6.—	18.—

Bones of Human Mummy					35.—
13 Human Heads (Mummies)					130.—
11 Human Right Legs (Mummified)					44.—
15 "	Left	"	"		60.—
3 "	Right Arms	"			15.—
1 "	Left	"	"		5.—
1 Crocodile Mummy (Hinder half of body)					15.—
1 "		"			30.—
2 "		"	Heads	12.—	24.—
2 "		"	"	10.—	20.—
4 "		"	"	8.—	32.—
3 "		"	"	5.—	15.—
1 "		"	"		15.—
Lot Small Mummy Crocodiles					30.—
Unwrapped [Crocodile] Mummy					10.—
3		"	"	@1.—	3.—

The total value for the Egyptian holdings of the emporium on January 1, 1878, was $944.75, one of the highest in the inventory; this figure does not include an additional $97.50 worth of Egyptian antiquities listed as part of Ward's private collection.[67] The record for the following year shows one fewer human mummy mask and a much-depleted stock of crocodile mummies. Meanwhile, new Egyptian materials had been added, including a third intact mummy coffin and an additional group of human bones from a mummy.

Ward the entrepreneur had clearly established a pipeline between Alexandria and Rochester to supply marketable antiquities with mummies and coffins "continually replenished, as sales occur." Over the following decade, it is possible to observe these stores of Egyptian antiquities wax and wane as sales and new acquisitions left their marks on the company's inventories. For example, when tracking left legs, we find fifteen in 1878, 1879, 1880, and 1881; then fourteen in 1884; ten in 1885; fifteen in 1887; fourteen in 1889; and thirteen in 1890. For some reason, left legs usually outnumbered rights. The inventories never list an even number of arms, and unlike legs, right arms were more commonly stocked than lefts. Most prices remained stable: mummy heads at $10 each, right legs at $4 each, and left arms at $5 each. Inexplicably, left legs increased in value to $5.60 in 1885, and right arms rose from $5 to $6 in 1890. Sometimes tendered separately were the skulls of Egyptian mummies priced from $12 to $15, a premium above the values listed among the in-house inventories.[68] Curiously, a mummified crocodile head was worth 20% more than a human one.

GETTING THE WHOLE STORY

For some reason, no whole mummies appear in these inventories even though some were definitely owned, exhibited, and sold by the company. It is impossible to know, of course, whether in every case a "whole" mummy arrived as advertised. For example, a handwritten contract in the Ward archives shows that he was obligated to supply an Egyptian mummy to the Louisville Industrial Exposition for the period September 7 to October 23, 1880.[69] Yet the inventory for January 1, 1881, lists an Egyptian mummy head ($10) and coffin ($150) "at Louisville." Did the Exposition get what only seemed like a complete mummy in its coffin? It may have been difficult to tell since the contract stipulates that Ward was responsible for building and maintaining all displays. More reliably, perhaps, Ward sold an Egyptian mummy and some coffins to the Rochester Theological Seminary (now absorbed into the Colgate Rochester Crozer Divinity School) as part of its Biblical Museum.[70] Ward was a close friend of the seminary's president, Dr. Augustus Hopkins Strong, a Baptist theologian who later published a charming personal recollection of Ward's adventurous life.[71]

In 1882, Cornell University reportedly ordered an Egyptian mummy and coffin from Ward's Establishment.[72] It cannot be confirmed, however, that these were ever delivered by the company. Cornell quite famously procured a mummy named Penpi at about this time, but contemporary accounts mention no involvement by Henry Ward. The *New York Times, Chicago Daily Tribune,* and other newspapers described the acquisition in detail, often quoting correspondence between the principals involved: A. D. White (president of Cornell), G. P. Pomeroy (US consul general in Cairo), and E. Brugsch (a museum administrator in Cairo who worked with both the Service des Antiquités and antiquities dealers).[73] One newspaper reported on its front page:

> Cornell University has ordered a mummy from Thebes. The mummy was once a Mr. Penpi, who was buried during the twenty-third dynasty in the Necropolis. What there is left of the gentleman is covered over with symbols and hieroglyphics to such an extent that Cornell is certain it has secured a person who must have been of great consequence in his day, though of little use now except for old junk.[74]

Within months of its arrival at Cornell, the mummy of Penpi was dissected before a group of 150 spectators and some of its wrappings were distributed as gifts.[75] There remains a possibility that Ward facilitated the importation of Penpi, but it may be that Cornell's order for a mummy from Ward's was dropped when Pomeroy secured the prize from Cairo.[76]

The best-documented example of a major sale by Ward is the intact mummy and coffin of Pahat.[77] Ward acquired these in about 1898. Both were sold in July 1902 to the Berkshire Athenaeum (now the Berkshire Museum) in Pittsfield, Massachusetts.[78] Based upon surviving correspondence, the purchase of this mummy and other objects by Zenas Crane, founder of the Berkshire Museum, was facilitated by an intermediary, Roy Hopping, a noted mineralogist in New York who bargained Ward's price down from $537.50 to $475.00.[79] At first, employee E. Ickes of Ward's Natural Science Establishment informed Hopping that Henry Ward had purchased the mummy and coffin in London, but he subsequently corrected that error:

> The mummy was purchased about four years ago from the Government Museum of Egyptian Antiquities in Cairo, Egypt, by Prof. Ward. It is supposed to be a mummy of one of the minor kings. . . . It was found at Sakkara, Egypt, and was said by the authorities of the Government Museum of Egypt to be of the XIX dynasty, about 2000 years ago, and is unquestionably genuine.[80]

Both Ickes and Hopping described the condition of the mummy in separate letters to the buyer, Zenas Crane. Hopping noted:

> The mummy has none of the face exposed and the covering is only slightly taken away. . . . The face below is probably in its original state. The feet are uncovered in part and are entire.[81]

Ickes added details about the best way to display the mummy and coffin:

We would take the lid off of the coffin and stand it so as to act as a background for the rest of the specimen, and would tip the under portion of the case on a slant so that the mummy could be easily seen.... We always kept it under glass when it was in our possession.... When lifting off the lid of the coffin, do same very carefully to avoid injuring the mummy. If the mummy has not been unpacked up to the present time, you will find that it is wedged in the coffin with packing of tissue and white wrapping paper to prevent damage from rattling. The head is detached from the body, and was in that condition when found, so do not judge that it has suffered any harm by transportation on this account.[82]

The packing papers remind us of the material found stuffed around Ankh-Hap, scraps that had led us to Ward's Establishment in the first place. It was clearly Ward's practice to pack some paper around a shipped mummy to help stabilize it. The detachment of the head is also a feature of both Ankh-Hap and Pahat.

Beyond Ward's correspondence, inventories, and sales brochures, I discovered evidence of his ongoing activities in scattered accounts. For example, the *New York Daily Tribune* reported in January 1896: "A number of mummy remains from the mummy pit at Manroloot [*sic*], Egypt, have just been received at Professor Ward's natural science establishment on College avenue."[83] The article points out that no whole bodies were in "this particular assortment," only heads and other detached parcels. In another story, a newspaper reporter recounted a conversation with Ward during which the former professor casually plucked a mummy's leg from a storage shelf:

"I want you to look at this foot," said Professor Ward, of the natural science department, taking out a mummy leg. "See the fourth toe; it is longer than the big toe.... Centuries of compressing the feet into shoes of unnatural design have altered the shape of our feet."[84]

Henry Ward, the scientist-entrepreneur, was busy writing a new chapter in the history of ancient mummies. He turned the tourist trade in souvenir mummies and mummy appendages into a wholesale supply business that aggressively marketed this macabre merchandise. Others, such as the Nelson Supply House in Boston, might advertise and sell "Mummified Curiosities" that were clearly labeled as reproductions, but Ward's Establishment trafficked in actual human remains sourced from the mummy-pits. In a widely circulated pamphlet titled "What Is a Natural Science Establishment," his company boasted that "the Egyptologist looks to us for his mummies and coffins."[85] His was truly a body shop. In the midst of America's mummymania, Ward sold not only the body parts of as many as fifty ancient Egyptians, but his company also advertised and sold whole mummies and coffins.[86] We cannot know, of course, how many of the mummified remains mentioned in previous chapters might have passed through Ward's warehouse. Notably, his stock may account for a few of the Frankenmummies, since any of Ward's customers could assemble a respectable showpiece by spending eight dollars for legs, ten for arms, ten more for a head, plus a few dollars for some genuine mummy wrappings to finish the job. Ward, in fact, kept a large supply of authentic mummy cloth on hand, for which there obviously existed a market. Ward's inventory for January 1885 lists $100.60 worth of mummy cloth; for 1887 we find $102.10, and by 1889 sales had reduced that stock to $75.60. For a complete ensemble, an authentic coffin might be added for another $150 or $175.

No specific sales of Frankenmummies have so far shown up in the company's records, but several possible cases do exist. For instance, correspondence in the Ward's archive shows that Orville Nelson Hartshorn, founder and first president of Mount Union College in Alliance, Ohio, overspent his budget buying artifacts to stock a museum on his campus.[87] He received from Ward in the early 1870s several large shipments that may have included the most famous of the school's specimens: a mounted gorilla and an Egyptian mummy, both of which served the advertising interests of the college and as the victims of student mischief.[88] When the Mount Union mummy was not on loan to various expositions and fairs, it was so ill-treated on campus that it was called "the much abused mummy" in the college's 1882 student annual.[89] Undergraduates made a habit of stealing the mummy from the campus museum, burying it, leaving cryptic notes for faculty as to its whereabouts, and then forming a mock funeral procession behind the exhumed body as it was conveyed back to the museum by President Hartshorn. Many years later in 1940, the mummy was X-rayed in the Physics Department:

> The x-ray revealed a most startling situation, for the mummy proved to be a 'dummy.' The interior of the mummy consisted of two-by-fours, nailed very firmly and wrapped quite tightly. The hand, the head, and the two feet proved to be actual remains.[90]

Similarities between the Mount Union mummy and Ankh-Hap are frightfully obvious, particularly the tightly wrapped combination of wooden braces with actual human remains. It is also worth remembering that Ward's was renowned for its staff of taxidermists, and that the term "taxidermation" was actually considered a synonym for mummification in the nineteenth century.[91] In preparing the legs of mounted specimens, Ward's friend William Hornaday compared from experience the shriveling of the animal's skin to that of a mummy.[92] Essential to the taxidermists' craft was a supply of pine boards (¼-, ½-, ⅞-, and 1-inch) and two-by-four pine scantling similar to the braces mapped inside Ankh-Hap.[93] The wooden armature created within Ankh-Hap makes sense as a stabilizing structure for a mummy placed on modern display, not for a body laid to rest (or to resume its repose) in an ancient tomb.

On July 4, 1906, Henry Augustus Ward died of a skull fracture at the age of seventy-two; he was the first person hit and killed by an automobile in Buffalo, New York.[94] His brain was donated to science. A year later, an ironic joke appeared in the *Berkshire County Eagle*.[95] It tells of a visitor asking what the BC number meant on Pahat's museum label, to which another man replies, "Oh, that's the number of the automobile that ran over him." No one associated the demise of Henry Ward with a curse of any kind, except perhaps for the scourge of the ubiquitous automobile.

The evidence gleaned from the archives of Ward's Scientific Establishment finally illuminated the unusual dossier of paper scraps found inside the coffin of Ankh-Hap. There is no doubt that the company collected and sold Egyptian mummies and coffins during the nineteenth and early twentieth centuries. The mummy now in the Houston Museum of Natural Science was almost certainly one of them, perhaps even the smoke- and water-damaged specimen salvaged from the devastating Rochester fire. At some point, the body was rigged with a wooden support system by skilled technicians to facilitate its display. Archival detective work had thus filled an important gap in Ankh-Hap's history within the larger context of the treatment and trafficking of mummies in nineteenth-century America.

Chapter 6

A Relic in the Restroom

In solving a problem of this sort, the grand thing is to be able to reason backwards.

—Sherlock Holmes[1]

REASONING BACKWARD

Contrary to popular belief, the purloined mummies of Egypt migrated quite slowly into the protective museums of Europe and America.[2] Well into the twentieth century, many mummies were still being marketed to all and sundry. They continued to travel as exotic attractions in circuses, state fairs, carnivals, storefronts, and other venues. They drew crowds eager to see and sometimes touch the body—or body parts—of a dead Egyptian, all the more if the mummy was said to be that of a princess, priest, or pharaoh. Before Ankh-Hap reached safety within the walls of a world-class museum, he was among those who were trafficked in camp-style shows, hyped as Egyptian royalty, groped by souvenir hunters, sold from hand to hand, and stored in hazardous surroundings.

I discovered this unfortunate history by heeding the advice of fictional detective Sherlock Holmes, who knew the benefits of reasoning backward. We must start with what we know and then work retrograde. I was aware from accession records that Ankh-Hap had arrived at the Houston Museum of Natural Science in 1970, before which he was kept on the campus of Texas A&M University in College Station.[3] Hoping to work my way back to the year 1914, the date of the papers found stuffed inside the coffin, I went to the mummy's former home and searched the university's archives for clues. Eventually this research illuminated the career of yet another extraordinary naturalist and collector, Dr. Mark Francis (1863–1936). Francis was appointed in 1916 as the first dean of the School of Veterinary Medicine at A&M, where he had been teaching since 1888.[4] His successful campaign to eradicate tick fever won him the impressive accolade "Father of the Texas Cattle Industry." He was also renowned for bringing to his university lecture hall an Egyptian mummy destined to be revered in Aggie lore as "the oldest man on campus."

I found contradictory accounts of how, where, and when Mark Francis acquired the mummy and coffin that were the focus of HMRP. Some old stories were patently based on faulty reminiscences. For example, an A&M alumnus who graduated in 1913 remembered that underclassmen in his day were required "to memorize and recite the Egyptian name of the mummy."[5] Yet this would predate the 1914 coffin stuffing that placed the mummy at Ward's in Rochester, New York. More importantly, the mummy had no name for anyone to recite until 1921, when it was first identified as "Anh-hr-h3cpj." The acquisition of that name is firmly dated by the faded letter that accompanied the mummy to HMNS. This document seemed a logical place from which to start reasoning backward to discover how and when Ankh-Hap arrived at A&M.

"ANH-HR-H3CPJ"

On May 16, 1921, Henry Ludwig Frederick Lutz penned a letter to Professor Oscar Melville Ball, a colleague of Dr. Francis at A&M.[6] At the time, Lutz was an instructor at the University of Pennsylvania, but he was soon bound for a professorship in Egyptology and Assyriology at Berkeley. Ball had originally written to Dr. Wilhelm Max Müller at Penn, asking for help in translating the inscription on the coffin. Because Professor Müller had drowned in 1919, the request was passed on to Lutz, who wrote to Ball:

> The inscription contains a formula for the offering of the dead; as far as I am able to read your copy it reads: (line 1) "A royal funerary offering to the Osiris, ptj-n-swt.t, great god, lord of Thinis (or: lord of the double-feather, i.e., the royal crown (?)) ---- to god Osiris (line 2) the divine lord of the lands ---- lord of p³(?)-rtt --- before the throne chamber of Amon Re (i.e. the chief-god of Egypt) (line 3) ---- to the god GEM ---- good house ---- to ---- (line 4) the great god of Egypt. Food, drink, clothing, all good things ---- (line 5) Anḫ-ḥr-ḥ³cpj the son of ---- pa-mes, the mistress of the house, justified, GEM-grt (?), justified, living for ever and ever.

The parenthetical question marks are all Lutz's, who suggested that a trained copyist might produce a better text from which to work. Some of the transliterations given by Lutz remain confusing, and it appears that Ball himself did not understand some of the notations. Hence, for example, the misunderstanding of the symbol ³ (a) as the number 3 in the recurring transcription "Anh-hr-h3cpj."

Professor Ball's particular interest in the mummy is not revealed in this correspondence. He was, however, head of the Biology Department and as Francis's colleague oversaw the collections of fossils and other artifacts on campus.[7] He is known to have procured three Babylonian statuettes for the college and to have purchased an impressive group of clay cuneiform tablets from a collector in Florida, all evincing a deep interest in antiquity.[8] We may guess the reason why he sought a translation of the coffin at this particular moment. Egyptian mummies were stirring envy and competition among rival colleges across America. In 1893, the University of Texas had set in motion a plan "to secure the mummy necessary to the success of every college."[9] In that case, UT in Austin lost out to Southern Methodist University in Dallas.[10] SMU got the mummy UT wanted, which was exhibited in the 1908 Texas State Fair and remained on view at Fair Park until 1913; afterward, this mummy was displayed at various venues on SMU's campus and is now on loan, along with its coffin, to the Dallas Museum of Art.

In 1921, St. Gregory's University in neighboring Oklahoma became home to a mummy purchased by Father Gregory Gerrer.[11] The purchase was made from the bankrupt Glen Island Museum of Buffalo, New York, and was falsely claimed to be the only mummy in a museum west of the Mississippi.[12] During the first decades of the twentieth century, Professor Henry Philemon Attwater had already displayed some of the first mummies to be seen in Houston, Texas.[13] Attwater, like Professor Henry Ward, was a respected naturalist known for collecting specimens and exhibiting them at major fairs and expositions.[14] Thus, mummies were on the move in Texas and Oklahoma by the time Ball sought a coffin translation, obviously for a more formal display than standing the mummy in back of a classroom. In fact, the A&M mummy was demonstrably put on public view soon after Ball received his answer. In 1923, a visitor mentioning both Professors Ball and Francis viewed the mummy on exhibition during a campus tour.[15] In 1926, high school student Julius Franki visited A&M and won an essay contest describing his experience, which included the highlight, "saw an Egyptian mummy."[16] For a youth group touring the campus in 1927, "A mummy in its original case was the center of much interest."[17] After organizing a community excursion to A&M in 1933, a party of adults reported to the newspapers the thrill of seeing the Egyptian mummy on campus.[18]

The mummy and coffin of "Anh-Hr-H3cpj" were displayed on the second floor of Francis Hall, as described in the campus newspaper.[19] This story offers one of the earliest accounts of the mummy's provenance and condition:

> Long years after his compatriots had lain him to rest in his pyramid if he was king, and in his common grave if he wasn't, prying hands came ruthlessly to tear away the veil of the grave. Eager fingers tore open the intricate and beautifully designed mummy case to see if there were treasures to be found within. Whether the riches were found is a matter of conjecture, for even the story of the mummy is lost.
>
> The mummy came to College Station from Wichita Falls where Dr. Mark Francis once bought the entire stock of a museum there. At first visitors were allowed to gather around the relic and to touch it here and there, but the great American pest, the souvenir hunter, plucked a piece of the fabric here and attempted to chip off a piece of the wooden case there. The mummy's toes were broken off, and now lie forlornly on top of some of the wrappings. The mummy, lying in half of his case, now is protected from the public's reach by an array of display

cases, and visitors can come within only about four or five feet
of the remains.

The writer goes on to mention the hieroglyphic inscription legible
on the coffin lid "despite stains of time and of wear." The mummy
was clearly in poor condition thanks to unguarded access granted
earlier by Francis, allowing souvenir seekers to help themselves.
In fact, the professor had done some fabric plucking of his own. A
small item appearing in several Texas newspapers mentions a visit
by Francis to the town of Liberty in September 1929:

> A small piece of cloth on display in a downtown show window
> is supposed to be 3600 years old. The cloth was taken from the
> body of an Egyptian mummy at Karnak, Egypt, and brought
> to the United States in 1891. The cloth was given Miss Estelle
> Meyers . . . by Dr. Mark Francis of the A. and M. College, inter-
> national famous research worker and archaeologist, who visited
> Liberty recently.[20]

How often Dr. Francis distributed such souvenirs during his travels
cannot be known, but the storefront display of this relic is very
much typical of the times.

These reports about the origins of the mummy are the only ones
published while Mark Francis was still alive and able, if necessary,
to contradict these three claims: (1) the mummy and coffin were
discovered at Karnak; (2) they came to the United States in 1891;
and (3) Francis obtained both items by purchasing the stock of a
museum in Wichita Falls. At first, I failed to find any evidence of
this museum. I reasoned that it must have been a relatively small or
temporary affair, perhaps a traveling dime museum having a range

of curiosities of interest to the professor. The attribution of the mummy to Karnak in 1891 was a common claim for many imported Egyptian artifacts. In that year, a major discovery was made at Deir el Bahri near Karnak, where the mummies of nearly 160 high priests were recovered. This find made news around the world, and no doubt many mummies were later assigned this famous provenance. For example, in 1894 a mummy displayed in a store window in Lowell, Massachusetts, was reportedly brought to America from Deir el Bahri.[21] Whoever sold the mummy to Dr. Francis could easily have invented or inherited this background story to attract buyers.

After Francis's death in 1936, other versions circulated about A&M's acquisition of the mummy and coffin. I uncovered a new and significant clue in the column "Know Your College," published in the campus newspaper in 1938: "This mummy, comparatively well-preserved, was found in 1891 in the great tomb of the ancient Egyptian king of Karnak. Dr. Francis and Dr. Ball acquired it, among other things, from a 'Chataukua' traveling show that 'went broke,' about 1900."[22] The association of the mummy with a king's great tomb is certainly more hyperbole, typical once again of the descriptions of many mummies arriving in America. What is significant is the reference to Professor Ball's role in obtaining the mummy, especially since Ball was in 1938 the appointed curator of the artifact and the likely source of the information regarding a Chautauqua show that went broke around 1900. The date is vague and rounded, and in any case, Ball did not arrive at Texas A&M until 1903, and the mummy was still in New York in 1914. Naturally, I searched through the *Wichita Daily Times* for any reference to a Chautauqua gathering in Wichita Falls prior to 1921, by which time the letter from Lutz firmly places the mummy at A&M.

THE CHAUTAUQUA CONNECTION

The Chautauqua movement grew out of the Chautauqua Lake Sunday School Assembly, founded in 1874 by John Heyl Vincent and Lewis Miller in western New York. Originally designed to train Sunday school teachers, the camp-style meetings became a major facet of social and cultural life for nineteenth- and early twentieth-century Americans starved for entertainment and enlightenment. The association soon sponsored gatherings around the country that attracted presidents, professors, governors, authors, actors, and evangelists as participants.[23] Significantly, Teddy Roosevelt called the movement "the most American thing in America."[24] Its traveling shows reached into rural communities, bringing lectures, concerts, plays, debates, and other forms of instruction to the masses. The organization published its own monthly magazine, *The Chautauquan,* which included reports on local activities, such as a "mummy tea" fundraiser honoring the donation of an Egyptian mummy to a public library in Cazenovia, New York.[25] The magazine frequently commented on mummies for the edification of its readership, and suggested mummy programs for local gatherings.[26]

American newspapers eagerly reported on these Chautauquan activities, and often advertised the sale of tickets to meetings being held far away in distant states. These gatherings were billed as "a great university brought to the doors of the people" with weeklong schedules of events. Based on my search through newspaper accounts, only one such Chautauqua was ever held in Wichita Falls, Texas. I followed its planning and progress closely. Anticipation commenced late in 1912 with a headline in the local paper that blared: "BIG CHATAUQUA MAY BE HELD HERE."[27] The aspirations of the citizenry were finally realized in July 1914. A large advertisement

in the town's newspaper on July 5 called upon readers to "INVEST A
FEW DIMES NOW" to attend; the full program cost only two dollars
per adult and one dollar per child.[28] The ad declared this "a mighty
little price for so much real enjoyment, inspiration and entertainment." After all, the promotion continued, "One small boy washed
dishes for ten weeks" just to buy his ticket. On July 8, the *Wichita
Daily Times* announced the opening of the event on its front page;
meanwhile, the supportive pastor of the town's First Baptist Church
issued a public notice that no prayer meeting would be held that
week "on account of the Chatauqua."[29]

Within days, however, this pent-up enthusiasm gave way to alarm.[30]
Although attendees were "thoroughly pleased with the excellence of
the attractions" being offered, ticket sales were falling far short of ex-
pectations. In desperation, the Chautauqua cut ticket prices in half.
When the operation closed after six days, the glass-half-full headline
read stoically: "ENTERPRISE FINANCIAL FAILURE BUT OTHERWISE
HIGHLY SUCCESSFUL."[31] This surely represents the "Chataukua" that
went broke in Wichita Falls, providing the opportunity for Francis
and Ball to buy the mummy and coffin as reported in 1938. Reasoning
backward, I had finally connected the dots between Rochester, Wichita
Falls, and College Station. To be certain, I sought corroborative evidence that Ward's Establishment had a history of supplying materials
to the Chautauqua movement. I discovered that in 1881, the newly
established Chautauqua Archaeological Museum purchased materials
from Ward's catalog.[32] The acquisition was arranged by the head of
the Chautauqua Archaeological Society, Reverend Dr. Kittredge, to
support the educational mission of the Chautauqua Sunday School
Assembly.[33] In 1887, Dr. Kittredge also secured on behalf of New
York's Chautauqua Assembly a large shipment of Egyptian antiquities
from London's Egypt Exploration Fund.[34]

The chronology was finally coming together in true detective style. Ankh-Hap had left Ward's Natural Science Establishment in about June 1914, packed with datable paper scraps, only to be stranded about a month later in Wichita Falls, Texas. Who had bought the mummy and coffin from Ward's cannot be established, but the customer no doubt intended to earn a profit by displaying these objects in the big Chautauqua. That investment soured due to poor attendance, disappointing everyone financially. Cutting these losses, the unnamed owner of the mummy and coffin accepted an offer from two Texas A&M College professors to purchase the artifacts. Relocated to College Station, the Egyptian ensemble stood for years at the back of Dr. Francis's anatomy classroom, surrounded by fossils.[35] As noted previously, souvenir hunters harassed the poor mummy and its coffin until Dr. Ball had them displayed, out of reach, in Francis Hall. Before doing so, the mummy was allegedly X-rayed to prove to doubting students that it was genuine, a common practice with mummies suspected of being fakes.[36] This X-ray could resolve many questions about the condition of the mummy at the time; unfortunately, I could find nothing in the A&M archives about it.

In Francis Hall, campus visitors admired the coffin and mummy during the 1920s and early 1930s. After the death of Francis in 1936, the mummy became part of a new museum founded in September 1937 to house the Mark Francis collection of fossil vertebrates, the Ball collection of fossil plants, and the S. M. Tracy Herbarium. Located in the Serum Laboratory, the museum's first curator was Dr. Ball himself.[37] In a story about the museum and its curator, a photograph of the mummy, enclosed at last in a protective glass case,[38] appeared in the *Dallas Morning News* on June 4, 1939. The caption describes the mummy as an "Egyptian prince whose name sounds like a short-wave radio station call letters." The reporter, however, then gives the wrong "call letters": ANH HR H3CJP instead of H3CPJ. As might be expected, the story further enhances the mummy's pedigree by attributing it to a find "in the Valley of the Kings at Karnak, Egypt, in 1891."[39]

Significantly, the photograph in the 1939 article reveals that the mummy still possessed its jaw even though part of the face has been damaged. Harm has also been done to the exposed left foot. An illegible placard may be seen tacked to the inside frame of the display case, near the feet. Perhaps these same two tacks were found affixed to the base of the coffin when I examined it closely in 1988. These steel fasteners have since been removed by museum staffers at HMNS. The tacks have a particular design manufactured by the Keuffel and Esser Company for use by draftsmen and surveyors. A products catalog search showed that this type was marketed between 1936 and 1943, fitting the chronology for use in exhibiting the coffin at the A&M museum.

In 1943, the campus newspaper printed a joke about some "A.S.T.P. boys" (Army Specialized Training Program cadets) asking a freshman where to find "Sully's Statue."[40] The now-controversial memorial for Lawrence Sullivan Ross, a Confederate general and former president of the university, was erected in 1919. The clueless student responds, "Oh, that. It's the mummy down in the museum." The mummy remained a campus fixture, but with a reported history as frayed and fragile as its wrappings. For example, in 1944 a new "fact" entered the mummy's biography when a reporter claimed that it had been "removed from the ancient tomb around 1873."[41] The selection of this date is unexplained. The writer clearly had no knowledge of earlier accounts and was unaware that anyone had ever translated the coffin inscription, claiming that "no one knows his name." By this time, both Francis and Ball were deceased, the world was at war, and the mummy exhibit was apparently no longer labeled for the public. That lapse was eventually rectified. In 1947, a campus news item shows a familiar knowledge of the mummy's name. The headline reads: "ANH-HR-H3CPJ—No, It's Not Morse Code—A Museum Mummy."[42] The author cites 1891 as the date of discovery in Egypt, but he adds that the corpse was that of "an important person, probably a tax collector, according to the inscription." Thus commenced the mummy's fanciful career as an ancient revenue agent.

The article's information derived from new placards propped inside the display case, as seen in a 1948 photograph.[43] The placard to the left, cited briefly in Chapter 1, states:

AN EGYPTIAN MUMMY

THIS MUMMY WAS REMOVED FROM ITS TOMB IN EGYPT IN 1891 AND BROUGHT TO THE UNITED STATES. IT IS THE BODY OF A PERSON OF SOME LOCAL IMPORTANCE, POSSIBLY A TAX COLLECTOR OR OTHER REPRESENTATIVE OF THE RULER. AN INSCRIPTION ON THE CASE READS:

"MAY THE DECEASED BY THE GRACE OF THE LOCAL GODS, WHO ARE LORDS OF THINIS AND WHO OCCUPY A HIGH PLACE IN FRONT OF THE CHIEF GOD OF EGYPT, AMMON-RE, RECEIVE FOOD, DRINK AND CLOTHING FOR EVER AND EVER."

THIS INSCRIPTION IS SIMILAR TO THAT PLACED ON A TOMBSTONE TODAY. IT ASKS THAT THIS MAN BE TAKEN BY THE GODS AND BE SHELTERED FOR ETERNITY. THE CASE SUGGESTS THAT THE MUMMY DATES APPROXIMATELY 2000 B.C.

The other label, two copies of which lie visible in the case, provides a longer translation of the coffin text, following almost verbatim the wording in Henry Lutz's letter of 1921.[44] The extra copy of this placard has no other purpose but to help conceal the exposed foot with its missing toes.

In 1949, the mummy (reported this time as Anh-Hr-H3cpt) was described as both "a gay old dog" and "a casual cat, probably a tax collector."[45] The writer continued in a playful mood about "Anh" the mummy:

> If anyone could be called a "wheel," Anh could. He rose promptly every morning at eight and a half candles and partook of boiled ostrich eggs and a handful of pomegranates. . . . Then off to the provinces for Anh, for he had a busy day scheduled on his Egyptian calendar. Back from the provinces promptly at nine after collecting one million elephant tusks, Anh prepared to leave once again for his riverside house, appropriately named "Pile on the Nile," to spend a day of drunken relaxation with a group of selected sphinxes. Later, much to Anh's anxiety, he found that these characters were demons at playing cards—such poker faces.

The Texas A&M Museum housed the mummy and coffin for many years, where both received accolades as exceptional showpieces.[46] Deeply embedded in Aggie tradition as the "oldest man on campus," it was in this period that Anh-hr-h3cpj lent his unusual name to the hazing of first-year students, who had to recite it on demand or be paddled.[47] A whimsical drawing of the mummy propped in his coffin giving a "thumbs up" sign, published in 1977, even added the Texas A&M logo to the mummy's wrappings.[48] Eventually, people proposed that he was the exalted tax collector for no less a pharaoh than Ramses II, or that he was royalty himself. Proclaimed one newspaper: "King Tut never visited Aggieland, but one of his relatives might have lived here."[49]

The student newspaper often urged its readers to visit the mummy, which was a popular stop for dating couples prior to World War II.[50] After the war, guided tours of the museum were available. According to a 1951 news item titled "Pretty Secretary No Museum Relic," about Mrs. Lucille Ethridge, this "charming lady who ushers visitors through the Museum" confessed her special fondness for the mummy, even though "Where the cloth has deteriorated and fallen away, the bone structure of the right arm and of one foot are clearly visible."[51]

Just a decade later, however, the popular mummy faced an uncertain future.[52] Even though praised as a public success, with some three to four thousand visitors a year, the A&M Museum had lost its state funding and could no longer find the private money necessary to sustain its operations. In 1961, the headline "MUSEUM FACES POSSIBLE CLOSING" was accompanied by a photograph of "the famed mummy" in its coffin, being admired by the museum's stenographer, Mary Anne Franklin. On March 13, 1963, the campus headline announced: "MUSEUM DOORS SHUT BY 1959 STATE LAW" with the lament that A&M might lose all the objects once sheltered inside its walls.[53] The Student Senate tried to intervene, but without success.[54]

LOST AND FOUND AND LOST AGAIN

The next dismal phase of the mummy's afterlife can be tracked through the reporting of a colorful, persistent newspaper columnist named Frank X. Tolbert.[55] For many years, he published the regional feature "Tolbert's Texas" for the *Dallas Morning News*. He wrote about all things Texan: cowboys, ghost towns, rattlesnakes, oil barons, chili recipes, and the increasingly elusive "Aggie mummy." In October 1965, Tolbert visited the A&M campus and asked to see the legendary relic:

I'd seen the mummy, or rather the ornate case years before. This was the mummy of a tax collector for a Pharaoh who reigned more than 4,000 years ago. And no one knew how it wound up in Aggieland. Some said that it was sent by an Aggie ex from Egypt, and another yarn was that a side show went broke in College Station and the school inherited the mummy.[56]

Myths about the mummy were clearly morphing and multiplying now that Ankh-Hr-H3cpj had no museum staff to support or explain him. The financially strapped Wichita Falls Chautauqua had become a defunct sideshow in College Station; Francis and Ball were forgotten.

Tolbert was told by university officials that the museum had been closed and its contents scattered about the campus. No one could recall exactly where the mummy and coffin had been stashed. Following various tips, the journalist set off in search of the Egyptian corpse. He made inquiries among the students he met, but none knew anything about a mummy. Professors proved equally clueless. After a few hours, the university's Public Information Office began to panic that Tolbert was going to publish a scathing column titled "AGGIES LOSE THEIR MUMMY." A small party of campus officials therefore joined Tolbert in the hunt. Eventually, the misplaced mummy and coffin were found stored inside a locked men's room:

> The beautifully decorated, but fading, case of the mummy was raised and you could see the form of The Tax Collector. The former internal revenue agent for Pharaoh is in pretty bad shape. Anyway, after diligent search, I found the Aggies' mummy. Incidentally, the Egyptian name of the mummy, once required learning for all freshmen, now seems lost to all recollection on campus.

There is no mention of the glass display case or the identification placards bearing the mummy's name.

Tolbert penned another column about the mummy in 1966, titled "Egyptian Mummy Needs Insurance."[57] Just months after A&M's mad search for their missing mummy, a Fort Worth museum wanted to borrow "the Tax Collector." Tolbert wondered why a $10,000 insurance policy would be required just to move the mummy, which had survived so many years among "college pranksters" with the loss of only one of his "fossilized big toes." The author still had no idea of the mummy's name, but he repeated the tale of its discovery in the men's room. In fact, he reprised the story of that "frantic search" many times over the years.[58] In 1969, he announced: "Aggies' Mummy Finally Escapes the Men's Room."[59] Revisiting A&M, he asked again about the whereabouts of Ramses's tax collector. This set off another exploration, much like the previous one, that finally located the mummy in the same storage area, although no longer locked inside the men's room. It was during this period of neglect that Ankh-Hap's skull was probably infiltrated by nesting mud wasps.

Three years later, the mummy made news once more under the headline: "Again! Aggies Have Lost Their Mummy!"[60] Frank Tolbert had stopped by Texas A&M to inquire about the mummy's latest disposition only to stir another search by staff and students. The search party determined that the tax collector was gone, loaned to some museum at the University of Texas in Austin. Delighted that the mummy had a good home, Tolbert was about to pen the story when word arrived that the mummy had instead been sent to Dallas or Fort Worth—no one could be sure. The frustrated journalist opined in print: "Actually, I think that the Aggies, if they no longer cherish the mummy, should give it to the Internal Revenue Service. For the inscription on the mummy's case says he was a tax collector for Pharaoh Rameses II." Alternatively, he suggested that the mummy be sent to join "the beautiful girl Egyptian mummy" at Southern Methodist University.[61] Two weeks later, the latest mystery ended when Tolbert learned that the mummy, once "an object of considerable reverence" in College Station, had finally been found at the Houston Museum of Natural Science, "where it has been hiding for a year or so."[62]

When in 1977 the treasures of Tutankhamun were touring the United States, Frank Tolbert told for the last time his story of the A&M mummy's disappearances.[63] He continued to recite a false memory of the coffin inscription and other fables about the mummy's arrival on campus. His version of the Aggie mummy remained from first to last a tax collector for Ramses II. Even so, Tolbert's ongoing curiosity and concern for the mummy was laudable, and his columns provide an important bridge between Ankh-Hap's eviction from the closed A&M Museum in 1963 and his arrival at HMNS in 1970. There the far-ranging mummy and coffin would be formally registered on June 26, 1985, as a permanent loan from Texas A&M University.

ANKH-HAP IN HOUSTON

The coffin with its shopworn and travel-weary inhabitant reached Houston in the company of the three Babylonian statuettes and seven cuneiform tablets once owned by Professor Oscar Ball, along with some of his fossil plants.[64] According to Carl Aiken, then the associate director of HMNS, "The [A&M] Museum Committee, which governed the use of the building, asked us to come and get these things so that they might be kept in a safe place."[65] He added that in 1977 "the mummy was not on display [in Houston] because of its poor condition." Safe but out of sight for many years, Ankh-Hap was finally placed on public view inside a new museum case in 1986. He has been a favorite among visitors ever since, and from time to time, as indicated in Chapter 1, the star of his own museum exhibitions. His was no easy journey, and newspapers have summarized the history of Ankh-Hap's life and beyond with a hint of regret: "When an Egyptian . . . died some 2,500 years ago, he probably thought his troubles were over. Boy, was he wrong. In subsequent years he was mutilated, mummy-napped and shipped to America."[66] In recent years, even poor Ankh-Hap has been apportioned his small share of imagined paranormal mischief. Local newspapers reported in 2006 that Ankh-Hap was brooding and angry. According to an HMNS security guard, the mummy was allegedly perturbed by the presence of another mummy in the museum, which was visiting the premises as part of a temporary exhibition. Until the rival corpse was removed, the museum was said to suffer a rash of mysterious technical problems.[67] Telling a reporter about his experiences with various frights in the night, the guard confessed in a hushed voice that the HMNS mummy terrified him.

Ankh-Hap frightened my daughter, too. Years earlier at the age of seven, she became alarmed that her father was working hands-on with such vindictive creatures without taking the necessary precautions. To her young mind tainted by modern cultural stereotypes, I appeared oblivious to my impending doom. As in the movies, if there were hieroglyphic curses on the coffins, I had missed them. If strange phenomena were following me around, I had not noticed them. If there were moans in the night and odd drag-marks on the floor, I had not heard or seen them. So, for my sake, she took matters into her own hands. I found her warnings inked onto a set of pages stacked neatly on my desk. Her first drawing shows me removing the lid of the coffin and waking the mummy inside. Nearby, a horrified museum guard—like the frightened one twenty years later—gestures dramatically at the yawning corpse. The next page pictures the mummy eyeing the guard and me, all three of us unsure of what might happen next. In the third image, the mummy wanders casually through the museum, with horrified patrons passing out along his path. Then, the final drawing shows the mummy driving away in a car. To my young daughter, this represented a warning I might finally heed, for the vehicle was my own, stolen by an unpredictable creature I should never have disturbed.

The long-suffering son of Maat-Djehuty never took a joyride with my car in order to exact his revenge. Notwithstanding what others have done to him, he has done no harm to those of us interested in his welfare. On the contrary, I would like to think that Ankh-Hap might welcome the scholarly attention devoted to him. In the end, Texas A&M University did the sensible thing in 1970 by seeking a safe new home for Ankh-Hap; the Houston Museum of Natural Science did the principled thing by accepting that commitment; and the Houston Mummy Research Program has done the responsible thing by rediscovering and telling his story. He has been reunited with his true name and identity, restored to his rightful place in history, and allowed to share his myriad experiences on behalf of millions of unfortunates like him. It is an old cliché of detective stories that the detective must speak for the dead. I have pursued this goal, mindful that while I have no right or reason to dig up mummies, I do have a responsibility to those that have been removed from their resting places by others. Some mummies do need rescuing. By doing so, I can only hope to turn Ankh-Hap's suffering into lessons worthy of his sacrifice.

Not the least of these lessons is this: mummies do not curse us; we are more likely to curse them. During the lifetime of Henry Augustus Ward, stretching from 1834 to 1906, ancient Egyptians became a profitable commodity in American commerce. Mummies real, manufactured, and imagined stirred the nation's fascination through newspapers, magazines, exhibitions, museums, university collections, and popular literature to a degree now nearly forgotten. Today, when we think about merchandizing Egyptian mummies, our minds turn quickly to store aisles stocked with mummy toys, costumes, candy, and comic books.[68] No one now expects to find genuine mummies on those shelves, either as entire corpses still in their coffins or as disarticulated heads and limbs for sale. Yet there had been a time when anyone interested in owning a piece of a real person could order from Ward's catalog a mummy's right leg for four dollars or a left arm for five dollars. Buyers could build their own Egyptian mummies from stocked parts and add authentic ancient cloth wrappings and a coffin to complete the ensemble. Ancient amulets and other Egyptian personal ornaments were also available for purchase. When today we watch a TV commercial for a plastic mummy figure "with accessories sold separately," we can scarcely imagine a time when actual corpses were marketed in the same way. Ward might have marveled at our reluctance to shop his bona fide mummy merchandise while also tut-tutting at our own commercial-ization of mummies as cinematic ghouls bearing grudges. He could scarcely believe that in the first decade of the twenty-first century, Universal Pictures would gross over a billion dollars in box office receipts for just three of its mummy horror movies.[69]

Ankh-Hap was a real person living in his own reality and not just a research project: *Mummified human remains remain human remains in spite of being mummified.* Those who study mummies today fall generally into two camps, the preservationists and the dissectors.[70] I identify most comfortably with the former group. For better or worse, I lack the medical detachment of a famous expert who remarked, "I just view a dead body as a broken-down car" while he carved up mummies with knives and saws surrounded by plastic garbage bags being stuffed with unwanted body parts.[71] Like Grafton Elliot Smith a century before, this anatomist was salvaging useful medical information in a makeshift morgue under difficult circumstances. Even so, harvesting selected fingers, ears, tissue samples, and other body parts from hundreds of mummies no longer seen as human beings does create an unsettling image. Curiosity, too, needs a conscience.

We now know that Ankh-Hap was no monster. He was just a man, an ordinary man who happened to live in a culture quite unlike our own. For that reason, some have tried to make him some*thing* and some*one* he was not, for example an accursed kinsman of King Tut. Today, however, Ankh-Hap is no less important or interesting simply because he did not really share the royal blood of Tutankhamun or collect taxes for Ramses II. He lies in state at a world-class museum (Figure 6.1), rescued from a restroom and studied as carefully and reverently as possible by people seeking knowledge of his world and its influence over ours.

Figure 6.1. The author and Ankh-Hap, 2022
Courtesy of Linda Holt.

APPENDIX 1

Houston Mummy Research Program Volunteers

Houston Museum of Natural Science

Elisa Phelps (Museum Program Manager), Curator of Anthropology
Lisa Rebori, Registrar
Truett Latimer, President
Terrell Falk, Director of Marketing and Communications
Stephanie Meeks, Development Officer
Dr. Richard Baldauf, Education Director
Donna Meadows, Associate Registrar

University of Houston

Dr. Frank Holt (Program Director), History Department
Gautham Sastri (University Program Manager), History Undergraduate Student
Dr. Rebecca Storey, Anthropology Department
Dr. Wulf Massell, Director of Cullen Image Processing Laboratory
Dr. Anne Simpson, Department of Computer Science
Dr. Harry Deans, Director of Enhanced Oil Recovery Laboratory
Dr. Charles Carlisle, Manager of Enhanced Oil Recovery Laboratory
Shirley McCraw, Analyst for Allied Geophysical Laboratory
Dr. Roosevelt Jones, Department of Biology
Dr. Subramaniam Venketeswaran, Department of Biology
Eric Miller, Media Relations
Cheryl Golden, History Graduate Student

Texas A&M University

Dr. Charles Schultz, Archivist
Jerry Cooper, Association of Former Students

Special Services/Consultants

Dr. Charles Van Siclen III, Egyptologist
Dr. Rosalie David, Egyptologist
Sam Valastro Jr., Radio-Carbon Laboratory of Balcones Research Center
Karl Kabelac, Rush Rhees Library at the University of Rochester
Henry Barbeau, President of Ward's Science
Melissa Mead, Rush Rhees Library at the University of Rochester
Dr. Mark Greco, Senior Lecturer in Medical Imaging, Charles Sturt University,
    Australia
Dr. Corletta C. Trejo, Dental Surgeon
Dr. Jonathan Elias, Egyptologist
Dr. Paula J. Reimer, Queen's University Belfast
Earthman Funeral Directors

APPENDIX 2

Henry Ward's Peruvian Mummies

Many people are surprised to learn that mummification was practiced in Peru far earlier than in Egypt, and that a market existed for the bodies of both during the nineteenth century.[1] Ever the entrepreneur, Henry Ward sought to profit from the sale of these Peruvian as well Egyptian mummies, although the supply and demand was always greater for the latter. In January 1877, Ward had in stock from Peru two legs and one head, plus a skull.[2] Two years later, the company still owned these items plus a second skull from Tinta, Peru, listed at twelve dollars, and an intact mummy from Chancay valued at sixty-five dollars.[3] In 1880, the emporium stocked two additional Peruvian items: a human head in a jar (twenty dollars) and the skull of a child (four dollars). All of these remained on the books in 1881, suggesting sluggish sales. Nevertheless, Ward acquired yet another Peruvian mummy in 1883, listed in his January 1, 1884, inventory at seventy-five dollars. This one arrived in Rochester via Paris, sent by Edwin Howell, who explained to Ward about a shipment of several boxes of merchandise, "one with *Peruvian Antiquities*!! I did not think I could be led into buying any such things but I ran across some good things so very cheap that I spent 300 francs mostly *nice* ornamented pots and a mummy."[4] In 1887, Ward still owned the two mummies plus two dollars' worth of mummy hair from Peru. The same inventory existed in 1889 and 1890, but the value of the first mummy had by then dropped to fifty dollars. The eventual fate of Ward's Peruvian mummies can only be guessed. The poem "As Others See Us" in the University of Rochester student yearbook for 1906 mentions two Peruvian mummies kept on campus in Sibley Hall:

> Well, sakes alive,
> Will you look there?
> The mummies

Over by the door
Where we came in.
One at each side
Behind a great big desk.
They look almost like life.
Come on, let's look around.
Hold on!
One of them mummies moved.
Well, I'll be dinged,
He's getin' down
And comin' towards us.
Gee whiz!!!
He is a she.
What does it say?
We must not talk
Nor breathe
Out-loud?
Let's go then.[5]

These may be the Peruvian mummies from Ward's establishment, given the close association of the company with this university. Another mummy, perhaps Egyptian, was on display in the Geology Museum according to an anecdote in the 1917 yearbook of the associated women's college.[6] Ward's profits from the mummy trade clearly derived from Egypt rather than Peru. It must be mentioned that he also sold Nubian, Pawnee, Cheyenne, and Sioux skulls at his emporium.[7]

NOTES

Preface

1. For this reason, some museums are now abandoning the word "mummy" itself, preferring "mummified person" instead: https://twmuseumsandarchives.
   medium.com/our-changing-relationship-with-irtyru-1919b68a7f5. The term
   "mummy" has a long and complicated history, discussed elsewhere in this
   book, but it is unlikely ever to be banished altogether from our vocabulary and
   it will be used here with due acknowledgment of its residual colonialist and
   pop culture baggage.
2. These themes are explored in Scott Trafton, *Egypt Land: Race and Nineteenth
   Century American Egyptomania* (Durham, NC: Duke University Press, 2004),
   and eloquently summarized in Christina Riggs, *Treasured: How Tutankhamun
   Shaped a Century* (New York: Public Affairs, 2021), especially 344–350.
3. Grafton Elliot Smith, *Catalogue général des antiquités égyptiennes du Musée
   du Caire N° 61051-61100: The Royal Mummies* (Cairo: Institut français
   d'archéologie orientale, 1912), iv–v.
4. Bob Brier, *Tutankhamun and the Tomb That Changed the World* (Oxford:
   Oxford University Press, 2023), 94–97 and 111–113.

Chapter 1

1. S. S. Van Dine (AKA Willard Huntington Wright), "Twenty Rules for Writing
   Detective Stories," *American Magazine* (September 1928): 26–30.

2. Transport services provided by Earthman Funeral Directors, story and photo in *Houston Texan*, August 5, 1987.
3. The numeral "3," for example, should actually be ⸀ and the letter "c" should be ꞓ.
4. For example, the coffin of Mes in the Denver Museum of Nature and Science was found to contain not his body, but that of a woman. For a case exposed by scanning, see Karin Sowada et al., "Who's That Lying in My Coffin? An Imposter Exposed by ¹⁴C Dating," *Radiocarbon* 53 (2011): 221–228.
5. For example, Frank Holt, *Alexander the Great and the Mystery of the Elephant Medallions* (Berkeley: University of California Press, 2003).
6. S. S. Van Dine, *The Scarab Murder Case* (1929).
7. On these documents, see further Chapter 6.
8. Arthur Conan Doyle, *The Bascombe Valley Mystery* (1891).
9. Arthur Conan Doyle, *A Scandal in Bohemia* (1891).
10. HMNS Accession No. 725, item 291 (two-piece coffin) and 292 (human mummy).
11. John Frederick Blumenbach, "Observations on Some Egyptian Mummies Opened in London," *Philosophical Transactions of the Royal Society of London* 84 (1794): 177–195.
12. Blumenbach, "Observations," 186.
13. John Davidson, *An Address on Embalming Generally, Delivered at the Royal Institution on the Unrolling of a Mummy* (London: James Ridgway, 1833); Thomas Pettigrew, *A History of Egyptian Mummies* (London: Longman, 1834). For context, see Kathleen Sheppard, "Between Spectacle and Science: Margaret Murray and the Tomb of the Two Brothers," *Science in Context* 25 (2012): 525–549.
14. Pettigrew, *History of Egyptian Mummies*, xvi.
15. Warren R. Dawson, "Pettigrew's Demonstrations upon Mummies. A Chapter in the History of Egyptology," *Journal of Egyptian Archaeology* 20 (1934): 180. The original Latin phrase may be found in Juvenal, *Satires* 14.139.
16. Judith Adams and Chrissie Alsop, "Imaging in Egyptian Mummies," pp. 21–42 in Rosalie David, ed., *Egyptian Mummies and Modern Science* (Cambridge: Cambridge University Press, 2008), 21–24; Rosalie David, "Medical Science and Egyptology," pp. 36–54 in Richard Wilkinson, ed., *Egyptology Today* (Cambridge: Cambridge University Press, 2008), 42; and P. Cosmacini and P. Piacentini, "Notes on the History of the Radiological Study of Egyptian Mummies: From X-Rays to New Imaging Techniques," *La Radiologia Medica* 113 (2008): 615–626.
17. Paul Cook, *Grafton Elliot Smith, Egyptology and the Diffusion of Culture* (Brighton: Sussex Academic Press, 2012), 9.
18. Arthur Aufderheide, *The Scientific Study of Mummies* (Cambridge: Cambridge University Press, 2003), 13. For an assessment of Smith's work, see H. A. Waldron, "The Study of the Human Remains from Nubia: The Contribution

of Grafton Elliot Smith and his Colleagues to Palaeopathology," *Medical History* 44 (2000): 363–388.

19. For an early examination of mummies in the Field Museum of Chicago, see the public interest shown in the *Helena Daily Independent*, December 30, 1923. For the royals, see James Harris and Kent Weeks, *X-Raying the Pharaohs* (New York: Charles Scribner's Sons, 1973).

20. W. M. Pahl, "Possibilities, Limitations and Prospects of Computed Tomography as a Non-invasive Method of Mummy Studies," pp. 13–24 in Rosalie David, ed., *Science in Egyptology* (Manchester: Manchester University Press, 1986).

21. Adams and Alsop, "Imaging in Egyptian Mummies," 25–26; J. J. O'Brien et al., "CT Imaging of Human Mummies: A Critical Review of the Literature (1979–2005)," *International Journal of Osteoarchaeology* 19 (2009): 90–98. The latter article takes a negative view of the scientific merits and methodologies of CT studies of mummies, but improvements are being made all the time: Sarah Wisseman and David Hunt, "Rescanned: New Results from a Child Mummy at the University of Illinois," *Yearbook of Mummy Studies* 2 (2014): 87–94.

22. It is a method still newly adopted for some museum holdings, for example the Pushkin State Museum of Fine Arts (Moscow): S. V. Vasilyev et al., "Anthropological Study of the Ancient Egyptian Mummy Based on the Computed Tomography Method," *Anthropology* 6 (2018): 1–6.

23. Zahi Hawass and Sahar Saleem, *Scanning the Pharaohs* (Cairo: American University in Cairo Press, 2016).

24. Some possible solutions to this problem have been reported: Frank J. Rühli, "Magnetic Resonance Imaging of Ancient Mummies," *Anatomical Record* 298 (2015): 1111–1115.

25. One newspaper columnist claimed overenthusiastically that Anh-hr-h3cpj' "may be the first CAT-scanned mummy in history." *Houston Post*, August 4, 1987.

26. *Houston Post*, July 30, 1987.

27. For example, *Houston Chronicle*, July 30, 1987, and *Galveston Daily News*, July 31, 1987.

28. The plan was to establish a permanent, accessible record of the original data, but within a few years these tapes became as obsolete as floppy disks. Recent efforts to convert this data to an updated storage system have been unsuccessful.

29. See Françoise Dunand and Roger Lichtenberg, *Mummies and Death in Egypt* (Ithaca, NY: Cornell University Press, 2006), 75, on mummies with detached heads. On the state of later Egyptian mummification, see Beatrix Gessler-Löhr, "Mummies and Mummification," pp. 664–683 in Christina Riggs, ed., *The Oxford Handbook of Roman Egypt* (Oxford: Oxford University Press, 2012).

30. Petrie's *Journals*, March 4–10, 1888: Petrie MSS 1.7, page 75. Available at https://archive.griffith.ox.ac.uk/index.php/petrie.
31. On Ramses, see Chapter 3.
32. James Douglas, *Two Mummies from Thebes, in Upper Egypt* (Quebec: Huner, Rose and Co., 1865), 3.
33. These were reported in Warren Dawson and P. H. K. Gray, *Catalogue of the Egyptian Antiquities in the British Museum*, vol. 1, *Mummies and Human Remains* (London: British Museum, 1969), numbers 19, 47, and 51.
34. Roy Moodie, *Roentgenologic Studies of Egyptian and Peruvian Mummies* (Chicago: Field Museum Press, 1931), 25.
35. P. H. K. Gray, "Embalmers' 'Restorations,'" *Journal of Egyptian Archaeology* 52 (1966): 139.
36. Gray, "Embalmers' 'Restorations,'" 138–139, citing the work of Elliot Smith in Nubia.
37. Moodie, *Roentgenologic Studies*, 23 and Plate XIV.
38. Dennis Forbes, Salima Ikram, and Janice Kamrin, "Tutankhamen's Missing Ribs," *KMT* 18 (2007): 50–56. See also Jo Marchant, *The Shadow King: The Bizarre Afterlife of King Tut's Mummy* (Boston: Da Capo Press, 2013).
39. For comparison, see M. J. Davey, P. Craig, and O. H. Drummer, "Dislodged Teeth in Four Intact Child Mummies from Graeco-Roman Egypt (332 BCE– c. 395 CE)," *Papers on Anthropology* 23 (2014): 18–28.
40. For example, Rosalie David and Eileen Murphy, eds., *The Life and Times of Takabuti in Ancient Egypt: Investigating the Belfast Mummy* (Liverpool: Liverpool University Press, 2021).
41. Odile Loreille et al., "Biological Sexing of a 4000-Year-Old Egyptian Mummy Head to Assess the Potential of Nuclear DNA Recovery from the Most Damaged and Limited Forensic Specimens," *Genes* 9.3 (2018): 135, https://doi.org/10.3390/genes9030135. PMID: 29494531; PMCID: PMC5867856.
42. Peter Der Manuelian, *Walking among Pharaohs: George Reisner and the Dawn of Modern Egyptology* (Oxford: Oxford University Press, 2023), 433, 669, 772. Reisner regularly paused in his archaeological work to read the latest fiction from Agatha Christie and other writers: 711.
43. Marc Armand Ruffer, "Note on the Presence of 'Bilharzia haematobia' in Egyptian Mummies of the Twentieth Dynasty [1250–1000 BC]," *British Medical Journal* 1 (1910): 16.
44. Mark Greco et al., "X-Ray Computerized Tomography as a New Method in Monitoring *Amegilla holmsi* Nest Structures, Nesting Behavior, and Adult Female Activity," *Entemologia Experimentalis et Applicata* 120 (2006): 71–76.
45. *Houston Chronicle*, March 24, 1989.
46. P. H. K. Gray, "Radiography of Ancient Egyptian Mummies," *Medical Radiography and Photography* 43 (1967): 34–44.

47. Giovanni d'Athanasi, *A Brief Account of the Researches and Discoveries in Upper Egypt* (London: John Hearne, 1836), 51.
48. Item EA6705.
49. Renate Germer, "Problems of Science in Egyptology," pp. 521–525 in Rosalie David, ed., *Science in Egyptology* (Manchester: Manchester University Press, 1986), 522–523.
50. Sowada et al., "Who's That Lying," 221–228; David and Murphy, *Life and Times*, 43–51.
51. The notation "cal" is used in radiocarbon dating to indicate a calibrated age and not a historical date.
52. Minze Stuiver and Paula J. Reimer, "Extended 14C Data Base and Revised CALIB 3.0 14C Age Calibration Program," *Radiocarbon* 35 (1993): 215–230; Paula J. Reimer et al., "The IntCal20 Northern Hemisphere Radiocarbon Age Calibration Curve (0–55 cal kBP)," *Radiocarbon* 62 (2020): 725–757.
53. Rosalie David, ed., *Manchester Museum Mummy Project* (Manchester: Manchester University Press, 1979); Rosalie David and Rick Archbold, *Conversations with Mummies* (New York: William Morrow, 2000).
54. See now J. A. Cockitt, S. O. Martin, and R. David, "A New Assessment of the Radiocarbon Age of Manchester Mummy No. 1770," *Yearbook of Mummy Studies* 2 (2014): 95–102.
55. Correspondence dated November–December 1987. See also Charles Van Siclen III, "The Mummy and Coffin of Ankh-hap at the Houston Museum of Natural Science," *Varia Aegyptiaca* 7 (1991): 69–79.
56. A later examination by consulting conservator Beverly Perkins in January 1994 detected traces of gilding on the cartonnage, which suggests a rather expensive burial for Ankh-Hap. Report filed at HMNS.
57. Van Siclen III, "Mummy and Coffin," 74.
58. A pilgrimage center for the worship of Osiris, located in upper Egypt.
59. A sanctuary in the Memphite necropolis.
60. That is, the deceased.
61. Van Siclen III, "Mummy and Coffin," 79.
62. Damages noted in the report of Beverly Perkins, cited above.
63. Report: Frank Holt, "The Ancient among Us," filed at HMNS. Article: Frank Holt, "Mystery Mummy: Unraveling the Remains of Ankh-Hap the Egyptian," *Archaeology* (November–December 1991): 44–51, and republished in Peter Young et al., eds., *Secrets of Ancient Egypt* (New York: Hatherleigh Press, 2004), 20–28. I subsequently published another version in my "I Witness History" series: "I, Eternal Bodyguard," *Aramco World* 71.2 (March–April 2020): 32–37.
64. Exhibition: *The Egyptian Mummy: Unwrapping the Mystery* (March 23–September 17, 1989), featured in *HMNS Museum News* (March–April 1989): 1–2.

65. *Houston Chronicle*, March 21, 1989; March 24, 1989; January 25, 1991; and September 3, 1993.
66. *Houston Post*, August 15, 1987. For background, see *San Antonio Light*, July 31, 1987; *Big Spring* (Texas) *Herald*, July 30, 1987; *Houston Post*, July 30, 1987; *Bryan-College Station Eagle*, July 31, 1987.
67. For a list of volunteers, see Appendix 1.

Chapter 2

1. *Houston Chronicle*, March 21, 1989.
2. *Dallas Morning News*, October 9, 1972; *Texas A&M Battalion*, December 4, 1980.
3. Agatha Christie, *The Mystery of the Blue Train* (1928).
4. For context, see Tosha L. Dupras, Sandra M. Wheeler, Lana Williams, and Peter Sheldrick, "Birth in Ancient Egypt: Timing, Trauma, and Triumph?," pp. 53–65 in Salima Ikram, J. Kaiser, and R. Walker, eds., *Egyptian Bioarchaeology: Humans, Animals, and the Environment* (Leiden: Sidestone Press, 2015).
5. The name Ankh-Hap is not unique. For example, a shabti in the British Museum bears the name of an Ankh-Hap son of Tadihatmehtyu (EA30005), and a priest named Ankh-Hap is known from a shabti on the antiquities market: https://www.trocadero.com/stores/Ostracon/items/1453246/Egyptian-Shabti-for-Priest-Ankh-Hap-26th-Dynasty-664-525-BC.
6. Nenad Marković, "The Cult of the Sacred Bull Apis: History of Study," pp. 135–144 in Mladen Tomorad, ed., *A History of Research into Ancient Egyptian Culture Conducted in Southeast Europe* (Oxford: Archaeopress, 2015).
7. Apis bulls were embalmed and buried in elaborate ceremonies: R. L. Vos, *The Apis Embalming Ritual: P. Vindob. 3873* (Leuven: Peeters, 1993). The ancient Egyptians also mummified birds, baboons, rams, dogs, cats, fish, crocodiles, and other animals.
8. Aelian, *De Natura Animalium* 11.10.
9. Nenad Marković, "A Look through His Window: The Sanctuary of the Divine Apis Bull at Memphis," *Journal of Ancient Egyptian Architecture* 1 (2016): 57–70.
10. Dorothy J. Thompson, *Memphis under the Ptolemies*, 2nd ed. (Princeton, NJ: Princeton University Press, 2012), 191–207.
11. As Herodotus famously declared in his *Histories* 2.5: "Egypt is a gift of the river Nile."
12. The reading of the father's name Padi is not entirely clear on the coffin; it may instead be Pya or Pamaa: Letter to Frank Holt from Charles Van Siclen III dated December 2, 1987. Sadly, one smudge is all it takes to erase a commoner from history.

13. Lissette Jimenez, "From Birth to Rebirth: Perceptions of Childhood in Greco-Roman Egypt," pp. 121–133 in Lesley Beaumont, Matthew Dillon, and Nicola Harrington, eds., *Childhood in Antiquity* (New York: Routledge, 2021).

14. Rosalie David, *Handbook to Life in Ancient Egypt* (Oxford: Oxford University Press, 1998), 313.

15. For more on these topics, see the lively presentation in Rosalie David, *A Year in the Life of Ancient Egypt* (Barnsley: Pen and Sword, 2015).

16. See Jean Bingen, *Hellenistic Egypt: Monarchy, Society, Economy, Culture* (Berkeley: University of California Press, 2007), 221–223.

17. Herodotus 3.16.

18. Herodotus 3.29.

19. On the Apis bull and desecrations by Cambyses and Artaxerxes III, see Aelian, *Varia Historia* 6.8 and *De Natura Animalium* 10.28 and 11.10, and Diodorus 1.85 and 16.51.

20. Stanley Burstein, "Prelude to Alexander: The Reign of Khababash," *Ancient History Bulletin* 14 (2000): 149–154.

21. Frank Holt, *The Treasures of Alexander the Great* (Oxford: Oxford University Press, 2016), 54–56 and 134–136.

22. This monument is now in the Naples Museum: Olivier Perdu, "Le monument de Samtoutefnakht à Naples," *Revue d'Égyptologie* 36 (1985): 99–113.

23. Or, alternatively, the Battle of Gaugamela: Ivan Ladynin, "Overseer of the Wab-Priests of Sekhmet Somtutefnakht: 'Collaborationist' or the Victim of Deportation?," *Vostok* 1 (2014): 18–28 (in Russian).

24. Arrian 3.1.4, with commentary in A. B. Bosworth, *A Historical Commentary on Arrian's History of Alexander*, vol. 1 (Oxford: Clarendon Press, 1980), 262.

25. Holt, *Treasures of Alexander*, 58.

26. Albert Wolohojian, ed., *The Romance of Alexander the Great by Pseudo-Callisthenes* (New York: Columbia University Press, 1969), 23–35.

27. Sulochana Asirvatham, "The Alexander Romance Tradition from Egypt to Ethiopia," pp. 109–127 in Philip Bosman, ed., *Alexander in Africa* (Pretoria: Classical Association of South Africa, 2014).

28. Wolohojian, *Romance*, 43.

29. Diodorus 1.46.7.

30. Diodorus 1.84.8.

31. For the Greek terms, see Herodotus 2.85 and papyrus 78 in A. Hunt and C. Edgar, *Select Papyri I* (London: Harvard University Press, 1988), 226 (P. Hamburg 74). The Greek term *tarichos* contributed to the naming of many coastal towns as Taricheae because fish were dried and preserved there.

32. Variously spelled *mumia*, *mummia*, *mumiya*, and *mummiya* in different sources. See Karl Dannenfeldt, "Egyptian Mumia: The Sixteenth Century Experience and Debate," *Sixteenth Century Journal* 16.2 (1985): 163–180; James Harrell

and Michael Lewan, "Sources of Mummy Bitumen in Ancient Egypt and Palestine," *Archaeometry* 44 (2002): 285–293.

33. Spell 154.

34. On what follows, see the accounts in Herodotus 2.86–90 and Diodorus 1.91–92. These are augmented for the period in question by a number of Egyptian texts: Mark Smith, *Traversing Eternity: Texts for the Afterlife from Ptolemaic and Roman Egypt* (Oxford: Oxford University Press, 2009), and Susanne Töpfer, "Theory and Practice / Text and Mummies: The Instructions of the 'Embalming Ritual' in the Light of Archaeological Evidence," pp. 23–34 in Katalin Kóthay, ed., *Burial and Mortuary Practices in Late Period and Graeco-Roman Egypt, Proceedings of the International Conference held at Museum of Fine Arts, Budapest, 17–19 July 2014* (Budapest: Museum of Fine Arts, 2017). Excellent background may be found in Salima Ikram and Aidan Dodson, *The Mummy in Ancient Egypt: Equipping the Dead for Eternity* (London: Thames and Hudson, 1998); John Taylor, *Egyptian Mummies* (London: British Museum Press, 2010); Howard Reid, *In Search of the Immortals: Mummies, Death and the Afterlife* (London: Headline, 1999); and in the PhD dissertation of Sofie Schiødt, "Medical Science in Ancient Egypt: A Translation and Interpretation of Papyrus Louvre-Carlsberg (pLouvre E 32847 + pCarlsberg 917)," Det Humanistiske Fakultet, Københavns Universitet, 2021.

35. Diodorus 1.91.3. Herodotus 2.86.2 adds that wooden models were shown to customers as samples of the finished product.

36. For further information, see Arpad A. Vass, "Beyond the Grave—Understanding Human Decomposition," *Microbiology Today* 28 (2001): 190–192.

37. According to a rumor reported in Herodotus 2.89.

38. Ancient sources reference an iron hook used for this procedure, but a recent CT scan of a Late Period mummy discovered what appears to be a wooden probe still lodged in the skull: Mislav Čavka et al., "CT-Guided Endoscopic Recovery of a Foreign Object from the Cranial Cavity of an Ancient Egyptian Mummy," *RSNA RadioGraphics* 32 (2012): 2151–2157.

39. Little care was normally taken with small organs such as the kidneys, bladder, and spleen.

40. Diodorus 1.91.4.

41. Diodorus 1.91.5.

42. On the process and meaning of these rituals, see Christina Riggs, *Unwrapping Ancient Egypt* (London: Bloomsbury, 2014).

43. Described by Herodotus 2.86.7 as "a hollow wooden figure shaped like a man."

44. The fullest surviving version is found in Plutarch's essay on Isis and Osiris, part of his *Moralia*.

45. This recognition does not mean that the sole purpose of mummification was to render the corpse as lifelike as possible; the process was as much performative as preservative: Riggs, *Unwrapping Ancient Egypt*, 88–89.
46. Salima Ikram, *Death and Burial in Ancient Egypt* (London: Longman, 2003), 200–201.
47. Attested in part by the information recorded on coffins and mummy labels. See, for example, Raquel Martín Hernández, "Faience Mummy Labels Written in Greek," *Zeitschrift für Papyrologie und Epigraphik* 208 (2018): 193–202.
48. In addition to the classic study by T. Eric Peet, *The Great Tomb-Robberies of the Twentieth Egyptian Dynasty*, 2 vols. (Oxford: Clarendon Press, 1930), also note Pascal Vernus, *Affairs and Scandals in Ancient Egypt* (Ithaca, NY: Cornell University Press, 2003), 1–49.
49. Françoise Dunand and Roger Lichtenberg, *Mummies and Death in Egypt* (Ithaca, NY: Cornell University Press, 2006), 133.
50. For extensive background, see Richard Sugg, *Mummies, Cannibals and Vampires: The History of Corpse Medicine from the Renaissance to the Victorians*, 2nd ed. (New York: Routledge, 2016); Heather Pringle, *The Mummy Congress: Science, Obsession, and the Everlasting Dead* (New York: Theia, 2001), 188–211.
51. For scientific analysis of some samples, see Barbara M. Scholz-Böttcher, Arie Nissenbaum, and Jürgen Rullkötter, "An 18th Century Medication 'Mumia vera aegyptica'—Fake or Authentic?," *Organic Geochemistry* 65 (December 2013): 1–18.
52. For example, Nicolas Lemery, *Traité universel des drogues simples*, 4th ed. (Paris: Laurent d'Houry, 1732), 565.
53. Ambroise Paré, *Discours d'Ambroise Paré, conseiller premier chirurgien du roy, à scavoir, de la mumie, des venins, de la licorne et de la peste* (Paris: Gabriel Buon, 1582); Pierre Pomet, *Histoire Generale des Drogues, traitant des Plantes, des Animaux & des Mineraux* (Paris: Jean-Baptiste Loyson, 1694).
54. Pierre Pomet, *A Complete History of Drugs*, 4th ed. (London: Bonwicke, 1748), 4; see also Paré, *Discours*, 7–8.
55. Sir Thomas Browne, *Hydriotaphia Urn Burial* (London: Chiswick Press, 1893), 80. The quotation is sometimes attributed to a different author than Browne; see, for example, Robert J. Kane, "James Crossley, Sir Thomas Browne, and the *Fragment on Mummies*," *Review of English Studies* 9.35 (1933): 266–274. For context, see also Philip Schwyzer, "Mummy Is Become Merchandise: Literature and the Anglo-Egyptian Mummy Trade in the Seventeenth Century," pp. 66–87 in Gerald MacLean, ed., *Re-orienting the Renaissance: Cultural Exchanges with the East* (London: Palgrave Macmillan, 2005).
56. William Gifford, ed., *The Dramatic Works and Poems of James Shirley*, vol. 2 (London: John Murray, 1833), 382 (Act 1, Scene 1); cf. Shakespeare, *The Merry Wives of Windsor* 5.3.18, where Falstaff imagines himself drowned and bloated: "I should have been a mountain of mummy."

57. *Wilmington Daily Republican*, October 2, 1896.
58. https://www.emdgroup.com/en/stories/powdered-mummies-used-as-medicine.html.
59. *Steubenville Weekly Herald*, December 9, 1881.
60. Eleanour Sinclair Rohde, *The Old English Herbals* (London: Longmans, Green and Co., 1922), 70.
61. Pietro della Valle, *Voyages de Pietro Della Valle, gentilhomme romain*, vol. 1 (St. Martin-sur-Renelle: Robert Machuel, 1745), 347.
62. Richard Savage, *The Poetical Works of Richard Savage*, vol. 1 (Edinburg: Martine, 1780), 101 (lines 235–236 in "The Progress of a Divine").
63. Nigel Jones, *Rupert Brooke: Life, Death and Myth* (London: Richard Cohen, 1999), 145.
64. Johann Frederick Blumenbach, "Observations on Some Egyptian Mummies Opened in London," *Philosophical Transactions of the Royal Society of London* 84 (1794): 195.
65. *Washington (DC) Daily National Intelligencer*, June 14, 1839.
66. Gervase Markham, *The Husbandman's Jewel* (London: G. Conyers, 1695), 35.
67. Henry Windsor Villiers Stuart, *Nile Gleanings Concerning the Ethnology, History and Art of Ancient Egypt* (London: John Murray, 1879), 90. Note also the report in *The Manufacturer and Builder* 2 (1870): 147 regarding this mummy-based industry. A notice about "Making Manure of Mummies" appeared in *Grass Valley (California) Daily Union*, October 17, 1872.
68. See "Egyptian Mummy Rags in a Yankee Paper Mill," *Wellsboro (Pennsylvania) Agitator*, August 26, 1858. For context, see Sue J. Wolfe, *Mummies in Nineteenth Century America* (London: McFarland, 2009), 173–200. See also her notice "Long under Wraps, Cataloguing Puzzle Solved," *The Book* 61 (November 2003): 4–5.
69. Quoted from the front page of the *Alexandria (Virginia) Gazette*, May 25, 1886, in a story regarding a "souvenir" mummy delivered to the chief clerk of the National Museum, Washington, DC. See also Wolfe, *Mummies*, 176–178.
70. Benjamin Radford, "Bailing in the Mummies," *Skeptical Inquirer* 43 (March–April 2019): 43. See also Grant Allen, "My New Year's Eve among the Mummies," *Belgravia Magazine Annual* 37 (1879): 93–105.
71. *San Luis Obispo Tribune*, January 25, 1879.
72. Wolfe, *Mummies*, 173 and 189.
73. *Somerset (Pennsylvania) Herald*, March 4, 1874.
74. *New York Tribune*, December 20, 1903.
75. *Bryan-College Station Eagle*, December 17, 1908.
76. "Techniques: The Passing of Mummy Brown," *Time* 84 (October 2, 1964): 114.
77. Georgiana Burne-Jones, *Memorials of Edward Burne-Jones* (New York: Macmillan, 1906), 114.

78. As argued by Chris Elliott, "Bandages, Bitumen, Bodies and Business—Egyptian Mummies as Raw Materials," *Aegyptiaca Journal of the History of Reception of Ancient Egypt* 1 (2017): 26–46.
79. *New York World*, June 3, 1890, and *Cincinnati Commercial Tribune*, October 16, 1904.

Chapter 3

1. *Boston Sunday Post*, September 10, 1893.
2. For a detailed list, see https://www.britishmuseum.org/sites/default/files/2019-10/British-Museum-Human-Remains_August-2010.pdf.
3. Alexandra Fletcher, Daniel Antoine, and J. D. Hill, eds., *Regarding the Dead: Human Remains in the British Museum* (London: British Museum, 2014).
4. John Taylor, "The Collection of Egyptian Mummies in the British Museum: Overview and Potential for Study," pp. 103–114 in Fletcher et al., *Regarding the Dead*, 103.
5. Angela Stienne, *Mummified: The Stories behind Egyptian Mummies in Museums* (Manchester: Manchester University Press, 2022); Jasmine Day, "'Thinking Makes It So': Reflections on the Ethics of Displaying Egyptian Mummies," *Papers on Anthropology* 23 (2014): 29–44; Christina Riggs, "Ancient Egypt in the Museum: Concepts and Constructions," pp. 1129–1153 in Alan B. Lloyd, ed., *A Companion to Ancient Egypt*, vol. 2 (Malden, MA: Blackwell, 2010); and Christina Riggs, *Unwrapping Ancient Egypt* (London: Bloomsbury, 2014). For an ongoing collection of viewpoints, see https://www.mummystories.com/.
6. Dennis Forbes, "Everybody Loves a Parade," *KMT* 32 (2021): 12–13; Christina Riggs, *Treasured: How Tutankhamun Shaped a Century* (New York: Public Affairs, 2021), 335–336.
7. I. M. Kaufmann and F. J. Rühli, "Without 'Informed Consent'? Ethics and Ancient Mummy Research," *Journal of Medical Ethics* 36 (2010): 608–613.
8. Paul Strathern, *Napoleon in Egypt* (New York: Bantam, 2007).
9. Although tasked in conjunction with a military invasion, there are things to be commended in the work of these long-suffering civilians: Jason Thompson, *Wonderful Things: A History of Egyptology*, vol. 1, *From Antiquity to 1881* (Cairo: American University in Cairo Press, 2015), 98–104.
10. Ronald Fritze, *Egyptomania: A History of Fascination, Obsession and Fantasy* (London: Reaktion Books, 2016), 175–179.
11. Benjamin Franklin to Vicq d'Azyr, July 20[-24], 1781, *Founders Online, National Archives*, https://founders.archives.gov/documents/Franklin/01-35-02-0220.
12. *Savannah Daily Republican*, May 20, 1823; John C. Warren, "Description of an Egyptian Mummy Presented to the Massachusetts General Hospital,"

Boston Journal of Philosophy and the Arts 1 (1823): 164–179 and 269–287. In 1767, the embalmed left hand of an ancient Egyptian woman had arrived from London: Maria Zytaruk, "American's First Circulating Museum: The Object Collection of the Library Company of Philadelphia," *Museums History Journal* 10 (2017): 68–82. For historical context, see S. J. Wolfe, *Mummies in Nineteenth Century America* (London: McFarland, 2009), 7–13.

13. Jonathan Elias, "General Analysis of the Mummy of Padihershef at Massachusetts General Hospital," Akhmim Mummy Studies Consortium Research Paper 14-1 (2014).
14. The assumed gender of most mummies was female, perhaps for prurient reasons. Early fiction works often featured well-preserved young beauties: John Irish, ed., *A Mummy Omnibus: 1820s–1920s* (Bridgeport, TX: A Bit O'Irish Press, 2018).
15. For instance, *Richmond (Virginia) Family Visitor*, May 17, 1823; exhibition advertised, e.g., in *Newburyport Herald*, May 6, 1823 and April 13, 1824.
16. *Maryland Republican*, June 8, 1824.
17. John Durel, "In Pursuit of a Profit," pp. 41–47 in William Alderson, ed., *Mermaids, Mummies, and Mastodons: The Emergence of the American Museum* (Washington, DC: American Association of Museums, 1992), 44.
18. Wolfe, *Mummies*, 15–32.
19. *Maryland Republican*, July 31, 1824.
20. *Alexandria Gazette and Advertiser*, June 24, 1824. See also Peter Lacovara and Sue D'Auria, eds., *The Mystery of the Albany Mummies* (Albany: Excelsior Editions, 2018).
21. *Onondaga Standard*, September 30, 1829; *Maryland Republican*, October 17, 1829.
22. *Cincinnati Commercial Gazette*, May 20, 1891.
23. *Newburyport Herald*, April 13, 1824.
24. See https://tennesseehistory.org/mummy/.
25. *St. Joseph Daily Gazette*, November 18, 1888.
26. *Graham (Texas) Leader*, April 26, 1901.
27. *Tacoma Times*, May 13, 1911.
28. Wolfe, *Mummies*, 89–93.
29. *Port Artur News*, September 6, 1929; *Timpson Weekly Times*, September 13, 1929. For details, see Chapter 6.
30. *Paris (Texas) News*, October 30, 1933 (news story and advertisement) and *Big Spring (Texas) Daily Herald*, November 27, 1933.
31. For context, see Andrea Dennett, *Weird and Wonderful: The Dime Museum in America* (New York: New York University Press, 1997).
32. For example, *New York Times*, May 27, 1880; *Boston Daily Globe*, December 3, 1884; and *Burlington (Iowa) Hawk-Eye*, September 4, 1884.
33. *Bryan Morning Eagle*, August 9, 1903.

34. *Rosebud County (Montana) News,* August 20, 1903.
35. William Fraser Rae, *Egypt To-day: The First to the Third Khedive* (London: R. Bentley and Son, 1892), 316.
36. Rae, *Egypt To-day,* 317.
37. Rae, *Egypt To-day,* 317.
38. *New York Times,* March 16, 1930.
39. *London Standard,* August 5, 1898.
40. *North American Review* (March 1890): 400–401.
41. *Bar Harbor Record,* June 5, 1890.
42. *San Antonio Light and Gazette,* October 23, 1910; *Washington (DC) Herald,* May 18, 1913; *Washington (DC) Sunday Star,* September 17, 1911, and March 18, 1923; *New York Times,* October 26, 1926; *Waterloo (Iowa) Evening Courier,* January 6, 1927; *Decatur Herald,* October 20, 1929; *Del Rio Evening News,* October 26, 1929; *New York Times,* March 3, 1935.
43. *Berkeley Daily Gazette,* January 4, 1935.
44. *Arizona Republic,* March 16, 1952.
45. *Bryan (Texas) Daily Eagle,* May 20, 1897.
46. *Logansport Morning Press,* September 23, 1921.
47. *Forrest City (Arkansas) Times,* September 20, 1895.
48. Widely distributed by the Associated Press, for example, *Salina Journal,* October 27, 2003.
49. *Boston Sunday Post,* September 10, 1893.
50. *Cincinnati Commercial Gazette,* July 2, 1893.
51. Described in his privately printed sales pamphlet, "Catalogue of the Theodor Graf Collection of Unique Ancient Greek Portraits 2000 Years Old Recently Discovered and Now on View in *Old Vienna, Midway Plaisance* at The World's Columbian Exposition, Chicago," number 94. See also *Thornton (Indiana) Argus,* July 1, 1893, with drawings.
52. Number 30007 in the Field Museum's Graeco-Roman collection.
53. Emily Teeter, "Egypt in Chicago: A Story of Three Collections," pp. 303–314 in Zahi Hawass and Jennifer Houser Wegner, eds., *Millions of Jubilees: Studies in Honor of David P. Silverman,* vol. 2 (Cairo: Conseil Suprême des Antiquités de l'Egypte, 2010), 305.
54. Jonathan Elias, "Overview of Lininger A06696, a Mummy and Coffin at the University of Nebraska, Lincoln," Akhmim Mummy Studies Consortium Research Paper 16-2 (Carlisle, PA: AMSC Research, 2016). Thus, Lininger AO6696 and A06697 joined a mummy previously given in 1885 by Henry Virgil Rominger (UNL 15-10-97): Elias, "Overview of UNL 15-10-97."
55. *Thompsonville (Connecticut) Press,* September 22, 1904; *Bloomington Weekly Pantograph,* September 16, 1904; *Philadelphia Inquirer,* December 20, 1904.
56. *Hamilton (Ohio) Evening Democrat,* October 25, 1905.
57. *New York Times,* May 10, 1940, and May 11, 1940.

58. *Chicago Daily Tribune,* January 1, 1942.
59. *New York Times,* March 8, 1903.
60. *New York Times,* November 27, 1909.
61. *Bridgeport Evening Farmer,* December 6, 1909; *Fargo Forum,* December 14, 1909; *Mitchell (South Dakota) Daily Republican,* December 15, 1909. For context, see Genesis 40.
62. *New York Times,* December 12, 1909.
63. *New York Times,* December 12, 1909.
64. *Chicago Examiner,* December 12, 1909; *Detroit Times,* December 14, 1909.
65. *Cedar Rapids Gazette,* March 11, 1979.
66. *Ottumwa Courier,* March 1, 1990.
67. *Abbeville (South Carolina) Press and Banner,* January 27, 1892. See also Heather Gill-Robinson, Jonathan Elias, Frank Bender, Travis T. Allard, and Robert D. Hoppa, "Using Image Analysis Software to Create a Physical Skull Model for the Facial Reconstruction of a Wrapped Akhmimic Mummy," *Journal of Computing and Information Technology* 14 (2006): 45–51; *Philadelphia Times,* September 7, 1885.
68. *Baltimore Sun,* August 17, 1895.
69. *Syracuse Post-Standard,* June 28, 1982.
70. *University of Illinois Daily Illini,* November 9, 1912.
71. *Abilene Reporter,* May 31, 1921.
72. *Houston Chronicle,* April 16, 1988.
73. Founded by Dr. Henry Abbott, *Catalogue of a Collection of Egyptian Antiquities* (New York: Edwin Varey, 1853).
74. *Brooklyn Daily Eagle,* March 2, 1859.
75. *Wichita (Texas) Daily Times,* July 12, 1912.
76. Samuel George Morton, *Crania Aegyptiaca* (Philadelphia: John Penington, 1844).
77. After his death in 1851, Morton's collection was purchased for $4,000 and then donated to the Academy of Natural Sciences in Philadelphia; it is curated today in the University of Pennsylvania Museum of Archaeology and Anthropology: Emily S. Renschler and Janet Monge, "The Samuel George Morton Cranial Collection," *Expedition Magazine* 50.3 (2008): 30–38.
78. Gliddon is mentioned in the poem "Opening the Mummy" by Benjamin Shillaber, *Rhymes with Reason and Without* (Boston: Tompkins and Mussey, 1853), 311, and in Edgar Allen Poe's short story "Some Words with a Mummy," *American Review* 1 (1845): 363–370, for which see Chapter 4 below. See also Scott Trafton, *Egypt Land: Race and Nineteenth-Century American Egyptomania* (Durham, NC: Duke University Press, 2004), 41–45.
79. *Milwaukee Weekly Wisconsin,* May 22, 1850.
80. *The Washington (DC) Evening Star,* February 24, 1923.

81. Frank Holt, "Egyptomania: Have We Cursed the Pharaohs?," *Archaeology* (March–April 1986): 60–63; Bob Brier, *Egyptomania* (New York: Palgrave Macmillan, 2013); Fritze, *Egyptomania*; Nicky Nielsen, *Egyptomaniacs: How We Became Obsessed with Ancient Egypt* (Philadelphia: Pen & Sword, 2020).
82. *Lowell (Massachusetts) Sun*, May 23, 1885.
83. *Oshkosh Daily Northwestern*, April 19, 1895.
84. *Anaconda (Montana) Standard*, July 28, 1895. This may be the same hand bequeathed years later to an Illinois college, where its fabulous pedigree was finally questioned: *Logansport (Indiana) Morning Press*, September 23, 1921.
85. https://www.invaluable.com/auction-lot/mummified-hand-of-cleopatra-86-c-1f3c692db5#.
86. *New York World*, January 16, 1898. For the question quoted, see Exodus 5:2.
87. *Iowa County (Wisconsin) Democrat*, December 2, 1915. See also *New Castle (Pennsylvania) News*, November 20, 1915.
88. Distinguishable from the composite mummies sometimes produced in ancient Egypt. See, e.g., Kiriakos Kalampoukas et al., "Crafting a Corpse, 'Cheating' the Gods: A Composite Mummy from Ancient Egypt Studied with Computed Tomography," *International Journal of Osteoarchaeology* 30 (2020): 114–118.
89. See, e.g., *Cambridge (Indiana) City Tribune*, July 26, 1888; *Wichita (Kansas) Daily Eagle*, June 27, 1888; *Rock Island (Illinois) Argus*, September 9, 1903; *Defiance Express*, August 14, 1906; *Portsmouth (Ohio) Times*, October 15, 1932; and even in a story about oil shortages: *Oil City (Pennsylvania) Derrick*, June 23, 1939.
90. T. G. Wakeling, *Forged Egyptian Antiquities* (London: Adam & Charles Black, 1912), 113.
91. *Philadelphia Times*, March 10, 1889.
92. Quoting a certain Zenas Madden in 1836.
93. *Corsicana Daily Sun*, May 17, 1927.
94. *New York Times*, December 18, 1929.
95. *Los Angeles Herald Sunday Supplement*, September 30, 1906.
96. *Corsicana Daily Sun*, May 17, 1927.
97. *Washington Post*, October 26, 1928; *New York Times*, October 26, 1928.
98. *Goshen (Indiana) Daily News*, July 14, 1888.
99. *Galveston Tribune*, June 8, 1904.
100. As reported in his memoir, *Perilous Trails of Texas* (Dallas: Southwest Press, 1932), 148.
101. Correspondence, Earl Dunn to Frank Holt, May 18, 1991.
102. https://www.henrysheldonmuseum.org/collecting-ethics.
103. *New York Daily Tribune*, February 22, 1887; *Brockway Centre (Michigan) Weekly Expositor*, April 21, 1887.
104. Wolfe, *Mummies*, 73–74 and 76.

105. Wolfe, *Mummies*, 202–203. The mummy may have been a bomb-laden dummy based on some accounts: *Daily Alta California*, January 2, 1876.

106. *Oakland Tribune*, May 3, 1914.

107. *Oakland Tribune*, May 25, 1914.

108. *Honolulu Star-Bulletin*, November 8, 1916.

109. *New York Times*, October 5, 1924.

110. *Berkshire County Eagle*, July 19, 1911.

111. *Alvin (Texas) Sun*, May 28, 1980.

112. *New York Times*, March 2, 1997.

113. *Port Arthur News*, August 26, 1996; *Nashua Telegraph*, November 13, 1996.

114. On this mummy, see also Andrew Slayman, "Corpse in the Curiosity Shop," p. 25 in Peter Young et al., eds., *Secrets of Ancient Egypt* (New York: Hatherleigh Press, 2004).

115. *Madison Wisconsin State Journal*, August 27, 1996.

116. *Naugatuck Daily News*, May 14, 1997.

117. *Orange County Register*, June 20, 1985.

118. *New York Times*, February 21, 1991.

119. *Syracuse Post-Standard*, July 4, 2003.

120. *New York Times*, March 2, 2011; for context see also Bob Brier, *Egyptomania*, 1–17.

121. *New York Times*, September 13, 1957.

122. *New York Times*, September 15, 1957.

123. *New York Times*, May 9, 2010.

124. *New York Times*, September 13, 1972.

125. These were purchased by the Rosicrucian Egyptian Museum in San José, California: Ron Beckett and Jerry Conlogue, *Mummy Dearest* (Guilford, CA: The Lyons Press, 2005), 151–152. See also https://egyptianmuseum. pastperfectonline.com/webobject/4260C363-CD2E-42A6-BD7A-37308 4409360.

126. On Palmolive's Egyptianizing ad campaigns, see *Waterloo (Iowa) Evening Courier and Reporter*, March 1, 1919. See also Day, *The Mummy's Curse*, 41.

Chapter 4

1. "The Unburied Mummy" (Harvey Comics) 1952, for which see Steve Banes, ed., *Mummies: Classic Monsters of Pre-Code Horror Comics: Mummies* (San Diego: IDW Publishing, 2017), 56.

2. For context, see also Sally MacDonald and Michael Rice, eds., *Consuming Ancient Egypt* (New York: Routledge, 2009); Charlotte Booth, *The Curse of the Mummy* (Oxford: Oneworld, 2009); and Joyce Tyldesley, *Tutankhamen's Curse* (London: Profile Books, 2012).

NOTES

3. Scott Trafton, *Egypt Land: Race and Nineteenth-Century American Egyptomania* (Durham, NC: Duke University Press, 2004), 124–132.
4. For a useful survey, see Brian Frost, *The Essential Guide to Mummy Literature* (Lanham, MD: Scarecrow Press, 2008).
5. For insightful evaluations of early mummy literature, see Nicholas Daly, "That Obscure Object of Desire: Victorian Commodity Culture and Fictions of the Mummy," *Novel: A Forum on Fiction* 28 (1994): 24–51; and Jasmine Day, *The Mummy's Curse: Mummymania in the English-Speaking World* (London: Routledge, 2006).
6. Albert Smith, "Mr. Grubbe's Night with Memnon," *Illuminated Magazine* 1 (1845): 31–35. Being locked inside a museum where corpses come to life became a common element in many mummy stories.
7. Smith, "Mr. Grubbe's Night," 35. Similarly, note the popular song "At the Mummies Ball" (1921), on which see Bob Brier, *Egyptomania* (New York: Palgrave Macmillan, 2013), 158–159.
8. Théophile Gautier, *The Romance of a Mummy* (New York: J. Bradburn, 1863), originally published in French as *Le Roman de la Momie* (1858).
9. Grant Allen, "My New Year's Eve among the Mummies," *Belgravia Magazine Annual* 37 (1879): 93–105.
10. Charles Mackay, *The Twin Soul, or The Strange Experiences of Mr. Rameses*, 2 vols. (London: Ward and Downey, 1887).
11. Arthur Conan Doyle, "The Ring of Thoth," *Cornhill Magazine* (January 1890): 46–61. For a similar plot, see George Griffith, "The Lost Elixir," *Pall Mall Magazine* 31 (1903): 154–165.
12. Edgar Allen Poe, "Some Words with a Mummy," *American Review* 1 (1845): 363–370.
13. Attending this imagined event is the historical mummy unwrapper George Gliddon.
14. Jane Webb, *The Mummy! A Tale of the Twenty-Second Century*, vol. 1 (London: Henry Colburn, 1827).
15. In fact, Frankenstein's monster is first described as a mummy horror: "Oh! No mortal could support the horror of that countenance. A mummy again endued with animation could not be so hideous as that wretch." Mary Shelley, *Frankenstein; or, The Modern Prometheus: The 1818 Text* (New York: Warbler Classics, 2019), 42.
16. Jane G. Austin, "After Three Thousand Years," *Putnam's Magazine* 2 (July 1868): 38–45.
17. Louisa May Alcott, "Lost in a Pyramid: or, The Mummy's Curse," *New World* 1 (1869), a work rediscovered in 1998 and now accessible in several anthologies: John Stephens, ed., *Into the Mummy's Tomb* (New York: Barnes and Noble, 2006); John Irish, ed., *A Mummy Omnibus: 1820s–1920s* (Bridgeport, TX: A Bit O'Irish Press, 2018).

18. A mysterious, deadly plant plays a role in the mummy's revenge, as in Clive Pemberton's later tale "The Bulb" published in his collection *The Weird o'It* (London: Henry Drane, 1906).

19. Henry Rider Haggard, *She: A History of Adventure* (New York: Harpers, 1886).

20. Arthur Conan Doyle, "Lot No. 249," *Harper's Magazine* (September 1892): 525–544.

21. Doyle, "Lot No. 249," 540.

22. Charles Mansford, "At the Pyramid of the Sacred Bulls," *Windsor Magazine* 3 (1896): 390–391.

23. Pseudonyms for Kate and Hesketh Prichard. E. Heron and H. Heron, "The Story of Baelbrow," *Pearson's Magazine* 5 (April 1898): 366–375.

24. Heron and Heron, "The Story of Baelbrow," 373.

25. Algernon Blackwood, *John Silence, Physician Extraordinary* (Boston: John W. Luce, 1909).

26. Blackwood, *John Silence, Physician Extraordinary*, 227–228.

27. Blackwood, *John Silence, Physician Extraordinary*, 240.

28. For examples: Seabury Quinn, "The Grinning Mummy," *Weird Tales* 8 (December 1926): 739–754; and Sax Rohmer (Arthur Ward), "The Case of the Headless Mummies," reprinted in *The Dream Detective* (London: Jarrolds, 1920).

29. Bram Stoker, *The Jewel of Seven Stars* (London: William Heinemann, 1903), and revised edition (London: William Rider & Son, 1912).

30. Bryson Taylor, *In the Dwellings of the Wilderness* (New York: Henry Holt, 1904), 174.

31. Ambrose Pratt, *The Living Mummy*, 2nd ed. (New York: F. A. Stokes, 1910).

32. Robert Spencer Carr, "Spider-Bite," *Weird Tales* 7 (June 1926): 735–750 and 863–864. For more poisonous tomb-spiders, see Seabury Quinn, "The Bleeding Mummy," *Weird Tales* 20 (November 1932): 625–644.

33. Jean Bodin, *Colloquium of the Seven about Secrets of the Sublime*, trans. Marion Kuntz (University Park: Pennsylvania State University Press, 2008), 49. See also Alexandra Küffer, "Tracing the History of a Coffin and Its Mummy: The Burial Equipment from Gamhud at the Museum of Ethnology in Burgdorf (Switzerland)," pp. 415–433 in John Taylor and Marie Vandenbeusch, eds., *Ancient Egyptian Coffins: Craft Traditions and Functionality* (Leuven: Peeters, 2018), 416.

34. *Omaha Daily Bee*, June 7, 1914. On this "haunted" coffin lid, see also *Holbrook (Arizona) Argus*, December 24, 1904; *St. Mary (Louisiana) Banner*, November 19, 1910; *El Paso Herald*, October 19, 1913. For background and discussion, consult Roger Luckhurst, *The Mummy's Curse* (Oxford: Oxford University Press, 2012), 25–60.

NOTES

35. For examples of other alleged curses: *Cincinnati Commercial*, April 2, 1879; *Mexico (Missouri) Weekly Ledger*, October 10, 1889; *Polk County (Nebraska) Democrat*, April 12, 1906; *London Observer*, February 28, 1909; *Washington Post*, September 17, 1910; *Salt Lake Tribune*, July 7, 1912; *Chicago Day Book*, December 27, 1915.
36. *Snyder (Texas) Signal*, December 2, 1921.
37. For excellent background, see T. G. H. James, *Howard Carter: The Path to Tutankhamun* (New York: Tauris Parke, 2001.
38. On the mummy curse, see Day, *The Mummy's Curse*; Luckhurst, *Mummy's Curse*; Charlotte Booth, *The Curse of the Mummy* (Oxford: Oneworld, 2009); Joyce Tyldesley, *Tutankhamen's Curse* (London: Profile Books, 2012); and Philipp Vandenberg, *The Curse of the Pharaohs* (New York: Pocket Book, 1977).
39. Some were unconvinced of Corelli's "mystic forces": *Danville Bee*, March 27, 1923.
40. *Cincinnati Commercial Tribune*, April 7, 1923. Many items were sent anonymously to the British Museum.
41. Scores of US newspapers carried this sensational story, such as *San Antonio Express*, April 6, 1923.
42. Frank Holt, "Egyptomania: Have We Cursed the Pharaohs?," *Archaeology* (March–April 1986): 60–63. For a more recent investigation of the so-called curse, see Mark Nelson, "The Mummy's Curse: Historical Cohort Study," *BMJ* 325 (2002): 1482.
43. Vandenberg, *Curse of the Pharaohs*, 40.
44. Vandenberg, *Curse of the Pharaohs*, 25 and 97, claims erroneously that Derry died before 1929 and that another victim, Herbert Winlock, also died before 1929. Winlock passed away in 1950. On Derry's mistreatment of Tut's body (and the mummies of the pharaoh's children, too), see Bob Brier, *Tutankhamun and the Tomb That Changed the World* (Oxford: Oxford University Press, 2023), 94–97 and 111–113; Christina Riggs, *Treasured: How Tutankhamun Shaped a Century* (New York: Public Affairs, 2021), 263–274.
45. *Moorhead (Minnesota) Daily News*, March 21, 1930.
46. *Syracuse Herald*, March 2, 1930.
47. *Chicago Daily Herald*, May 12, 1939. This endocrinologist, Jean Brochet, does not seem to have played any part in the excavation of the tomb.
48. Rex Keating, *The Trumpets of Tutankhamun: Adventures of a Radio Pioneer in the Middle East* (Basingstoke: Fisher Miller, 1999), discusses the so-called curse unleashed by the trumpet. See also Frank Holt, "I, Horn of Africa," *Aramco World* 69 (January–February 2018): 26–31.
49. *Xenia (Ohio) Daily Gazette*, January 13, 1982.
50. On this assertion, see Holt, "Egyptomania," 63.

51. Clark Ashton Smith, *Ebony and Crystal: Poems in Verse and Prose* (Auburn, CA: Auburn Journal, 1922), 83.

52. Adam Shirk, "Osiris: The Weird Tale of an Egyptian Mummy," *Weird Tales* 1 (June 1923): 55–56.

53. H. P. Lovecraft and Harry Houdini, "Imprisoned with the Pharaohs," *Weird Tales* 4 (May–July 1924): 9.

54. Lovecraft and Houdini, "Imprisoned with the Pharaohs," 9.

55. Frost, *Essential Guide*, 26.

56. Examples: William Everson, *Classics of the Horror Film* (Secaucus, NJ: Citadel, 1974); Thomas Aylesworth, *Movie Monsters* (Philadelphia: Lippincott, 1975); Donald Glut, *Classic Movie Monsters* (London: Scarecrow, 1978); Leslie Halliwell, *The Dead That Walk* (London: Grafton, 1986); and Andy Black, *The Dead Walk* (London: Noir, 2000).

57. *King Tut-Ankh-Amen's Eighth Wife* (1923), directed by Andrew Remo.

58. Some romantic/comic films: *His Egyptian Affinity* (1915); *Tut-Tut and His Terrible Tomb* (1923); and the Three Stooges in *We Want Our Mummy* (1938). For plots, characters, and other information on films and television, consult the Internet Movie Database (IMDb).

59. Kevin McGeough, "Heroes, Mummies, and Treasure: Near Eastern Archaeology in the Movies," *Near Eastern Archaeology* 69 (2006): 174–185; Stuart Smith, "Unwrapping the Mummy: Hollywood Fantasies, Egyptian Realities," pp. 16–33 in Julie M. Schablitsky, ed., *Box Office Archaeology: Refining Hollywood's Portrayals of the Past* (Walnut Creek, CA: Left Coast Press, 2007). Basil Glynn offers a different view stressing the diversity of mummies in the protean horror genre: *The Mummy on Screen: Orientalism and Monstrosity in Horror Cinema* (London: Bloomsbury Academic, 2020).

60. "Ultraman—Cry of the Mummy" aired on October 2, 1966. Laser eyes had already been introduced by Dell Comics in 1962, for which see the section "Heroes and Horrors" below.

61. Trafton, *Egypt Land*, and Day, *The Mummy's Curse*, provide in-depth treatments of these issues.

62. Hasbro G.I. Joe Adventure Team, "Secret of the Mummy's Tomb."

63. For numerous illustrations, see Banes, *Mummies*.

64. See, e.g., Bob Brier and Daniel Friedman, "Ancient Egypt in the Comics," *Kmt* 32 (Fall 2021): 56–67.

65. Jay Disbrow, "The Mummy's Hand," *Ghostly Weird Stories* 120 (September 1953): 1–9.

66. "Van Helsing vs. the Mummy of Amun Ra," written by Pat Shand with art by Marc Rosete and Walter Pereyra (Zenescope Entertainment, 2017).

67. "Spooked," episode 5 of season 8 that originally aired on NBC on October 27, 2011.

68. For an alleged warning ignored: *Miami Daily News Record*, July 23, 1930.

Chapter 5

1. *Ward's Scientific Catalogue of Systematic Collections and Individual Specimens of Geology and Lithology*, 2nd ed. (1891). See the same advertisement in *Ward's Natural Science Bulletin* 1.1 (1881): 15; 1.2 (1882): 6; 1.3 (1882): 6; 1.4 (1882): 6; 2.2 (1883): 6; 3.1 (1884): 5; 3.2 (1884): 6; 4 (1886): 7.
2. Arthur Conan Doyle, *The Bascombe Valley Mystery* (1891).
3. Branislav Anđelković and Jonathan Elias, "CT Scan of Nesmin from Akhmim: New Data on the Belgrade Mummy," *Issues in Ethnology and Anthropology* 16 (2021): 761–794.
4. Correspondence between Frank Holt, Elisa Phelps, and Henry Barbeau, February–March 1988.
5. His obituary appeared in the *Rochester Democrat and Chronicle*, January 6, 1944, and in *Ward's Natural Science Bulletin* 17 (1944): 58. See also Robert Vance, "Memorial of George Letchworth English," *American Mineralogist* 30 (1945): 130–134.
6. Douglas Sterrett, "A New Type of Calcite from the Joplin Mining District," *American Journal of Science* 18 (1904): 73–76.
7. *Bisbee Daily Review*, July 27, 1915.
8. Correspondence between Frank Holt, Elisa Phelps, and Karl Kabelac, March 1988.
9. *Bryan-College Station Eagle*, January 30, 1988.
10. Roswell Ward, *Henry A. Ward: Museum Builder in America* (Rochester, NY: Rochester Historical Society, 1948), 141–153.
11. Ward, *Henry A. Ward*, 50–58.
12. Herman L. Fairchild, "Ward's Natural Science Establishment," *Scientific Monthly* 26 (May 1928): 468–471; Mark V. Barrow Jr., "The Specimen Dealer: Entrepreneurial Natural History in America's Gilded Age," *Journal of the History of Biology* 33 (Winter 2000): 493–534; Sally Gregory Kohlstedt, "Henry A. Ward: The Merchant Naturalist and American Museum Development," *Journal of the Society for the Bibliography of Natural History* 9 (1980): 647–661; Henri Reiling and Tat'jána Spunarová, "Václav Frič (1839–1916) and His Influence on Collecting Natural History," *Journal of the History of Collections* 17 (2005): 27.
13. Ward's Natural Science Establishment, "Eighty Natural Science Cabinets," AW23 Ward (Henry Augustus) Papers (Rare Books, Special Collections and Preservation, River Campus Libraries, University of Rochester), Ward Project (hereafter Ward Papers), accessed May 23, 2021, https://wardproject.org/items/show/9359.
14. Ward, "Month-by-month journal, 1854–1896," Ward Papers, accessed November 28, 2022, https://wardproject.org/items/show/16062.

15. William Hornaday, "The King of Museum Builders," *Commercial Travelers' Home Magazine* 6 (February 1896): 148; Stephen Nash and Gary Feinman, eds., *Curators, Collections, and Contexts: Anthropology at the Field Museum, 1893–2002* (Chicago: Field Museum, 2003), 55.
16. Andrew McClellan, "P. T. Barnum, Jumbo the Elephant, and the Barnum Museum of Natural History at Tufts University," *Journal of the History of Collections* 24 (2012): 45–62. On the promise of Jumbo's remains to Ward's Establishment, see William T. Hornaday, letter to Ward, Ward Papers, accessed November 28, 2022, https://wardproject.org/items/show/15110. All citations herein of Ward's correspondence are derived from the Ward Papers. I thank Melissa S. Mead, the John M. and Barbara Keil University Archivist and Rochester Collections Librarian, for her invaluable assistance.
17. John Sutherland, *Jumbo: The Unauthorized Biography of a Victorian Sensation* (London: Aurum Press, 2014), 141–152.
18. *Ward's Natural Science Bulletin* 4 (1886): 10–11.
19. Only one passing reference to Ward appears in S. J. Wolfe's seminal work *Mummies in Nineteenth Century America* (London: McFarland, 2009), 237.
20. On these pits, see Colonel Straton, "Account of the Sepulchral Caverns of Egypt," *Boston Journal of Philosophy and the Arts* 1 (1823): 48–53; and the front page of *Hickman (Kentucky) Courier*, November 2, 1877. For context, see Tessa Baber, "Early Travellers and the Animal 'Mummy Pits' of Egypt," pp. 67–86 in Stéphanie Porcier, Salima Ikram, and Stéphane Pasquali, eds., *Creatures of Earth, Water, and Sky* (Leiden: Sidestone Press, 2019); and Baber, "Ancient Corpses as Curiosities: Mummymania in the Age of Early Travel," *Journal of Ancient Egyptian Interconnections* 8 (2016): 60–93.
21. Ward describes the circumstances in a letter to his aunt Susan Ward Selden (Marseille, December 6, 1854). See also Ward, *Henry A. Ward*, 62–83.
22. Henry Augustus Ward, Letter to Elizabeth D. Ward (On the Nile, December 30, 1854).
23. Ward, "Line-a-Day diary of Henry Augustus Ward" (henceforth, HAW Diary), Ward Papers. On the last if these sites, see T. Zimmer, *Les Grottes des crocodiles de Maabdah* (San Antonio, TX: Van Siclen, 1987).
24. Giovanni Belzoni, *Narrative of the Operations and Recent Discoveries within the Pyramids, Temples, Tombs, and Excavations, in Egypt and Nubia* (London: John Murray, 1820), 157. On ventures into the mummy-pits a century earlier, see Christian Hertzog, *Essay de mumio-graphie* (Gotha: Jean Reyher, 1718), 45–52.
25. "Horrors of a Mummy Pit," *Detroit Free Press*, May 25, 1867.
26. Thomas Legh, *Narrative of a Journey in Egypt and the Country beyond the Cataracts* (London: John Murray, 1816), 107–108.
27. Legh, *Narrative of a Journey*, 109–123.

28. Ward refers here to the plight of Thomas Legh, but gives the wrong date, a common error made also by Baber, "Early Travellers," 74, who puts the incident in 1816 rather than 1813.

29. Henry Windsor Villiers Stuart, *Nile Gleanings Concerning the Ethnology, History and Art of Ancient Egypt* (London: John Murray, 1879), 87–91, provides a very similar account of these mummy-pits, including the story of a deadly fire accidentally set by earlier visitors.

30. Henry Augustus Ward, letter to Chester Dewey (June 20, 1855). My own transcription of this letter differs somewhat from the redacted version in Ward, *Henry A. Ward*, 193–195.

31. Levi Ward, letter to Henry Ward (June 8, 1855).

32. Henry Augustus Ward, letter to Elizabeth D. Ward (Thebes, February 10 and 18, 1855), and letter to Susan Ward Selden (Cairo, April 16, 1855).

33. Isabella Romer, *A Pilgrimage to the Temples and Tombs of Egypt, Nubia, and Palestine in 1845–6*, vol. 1 (London: Richard Bentley, 1846), 293.

34. *Birmingham Age-Herald*, June 17, 1906, as reported by traveler George Ade. Heads were being sold to tourists for about a dollar each.

35. *Bismarck Weekly Tribune*, March 23, 1894, as reported by H. R. Porter.

36. Bob Brier, *Tutankhamun and the Tomb That Changed the World* (Oxford: Oxford University Press, 2023), 241.

37. Jason Thompson, *Wonderful Things: A History of Egyptology*, vol. 1: *From Antiquity to 1881* (Cairo: American University in Cairo Press, 2015), 223–229.

38. The weight is reported in a letter to his friend James Orton (April 17, 1855). See also the end of his letter to Dewey (June 20, 1855).

39. On April 13, 1855. He had already packed some of his antiquities on April 9. Ward later mentioned to a friend his shipments to New York: letter to James Orton (July 25, 1855).

40. Amelia Edwards, "Lying in State in Cairo," *Harper's New Monthly Magazine* 65 (1882): 200. See also *New York Times*, June 25, 1882.

41. Edwards, "Lying in State," 200.

42. *Baltimore Sun*, June 18, 1896. The illicit traffic continues today. In 2019, for example, an airline passenger bound for Belgium tried to board a flight from Egypt with the body parts of six mummies stashed inside a hollowed stereo speaker: https://www.cnet.com/news/mummy-smuggler-busted-with-remains-hidden-inside-speakers/.

43. Amelia Edwards, *A Thousand Miles Up the Nile*, 2nd ed. (London: Routledge, 1890; reprint 2008), 51. For a contrary view on "mummy scavengers," see Charles Lushington, *Narrative of a Journey from Calcutta to Europe, by Way of Egypt in the Years 1827 and 1828* (London: John Murray, 1829), 83–86.

44. Ward, *Henry A. Ward*, 157–158; HAW Diary for October 9, 1869, and Ward's Natural Science Establishment, "Eighty Natural Science Cabinets," Ward Papers, accessed May 23, 2021, https://wardproject.org/items/show/9359.

45. Ward's Natural Science Establishment, "Inventory A (1869-09-03)," Ward Papers, accessed May 26, 2021, https://wardproject.org/items/show/13224, and Ward's Natural Science Establishment, "Inventory B (1869-09-03)," Ward Papers, accessed May 26, 2021, https://wardproject.org/items/show/13225. The Egyptian materials are valued therein at $500.

46. Ward, *Henry A. Ward*, 157.

47. HAW Diary for October 10. In subsequent days, he notes meeting with insurance adjusters.

48. Ward, "Month-by-month journal, 1854–1896," for October 1869.

49. *New York Herald*, October 10, 1869.

50. Ward, *Henry A. Ward*, 158.

51. The controversy arose from Hornaday's cruel and racist exhibition of a Mbuti man named Ota Benga in the zoo's Monkey House, where he wrestled in a cage with an orangutan. See Pamela Newkirk, *Spectacle: The Astonishing Life of Ota Benga* (New York: Amistad, 2015).

52. Hornaday, "King of Museum Builders," 147 and 152.

53. For the story of this obelisk, see Bob Brier, *Egyptomania* (New York: Palgrave Macmillan, 2013), 111–150.

54. Elbert Farman, *Along the Nile with General Grant* (New York: Grafton Press, 1904), 85–90.

55. Sir John Gardner Wilkinson, *A Handbook for Travelers in Egypt*, 5th ed. (London: John Murray, 1876), 367.

56. *New York Daily Ledger*, June 14, 1850. For another estimate, see Aidan and Eve Cockburn, eds., *Mummies, Diseases, and Ancient Cultures* (Cambridge: Cambridge University Press, 1983), 3–4.

57. Stuart, *Nile Gleanings*, 91.

58. Petrie's *Journals*, March 4–10, 1888: Petrie MSS 1.7, page 74. Available at https://archive.griffith.ox.ac.uk/index.php/petrie.

59. Farman, *Along the Nile*, 88–89.

60. Stuart, *Nile Gleanings*, 87.

61. William T. Hornaday, *Two Years in the Jungle: The Experiences of a Hunter and Naturalist in India, Ceylon, the Malay Peninsula and Borneo* (London: Kegan Paul, Trench, 1885), 13.

62. Hornaday, *Two Years*, 14.

63. Hornaday, "King of Museum Builders," 149.

64. Henry Augustus Ward, letter to Lewis Brooks (February 6, 1877).

65. For these inventories, see for example Ward and Howell, "Inventory (1878-01-01)," D258 Ward's Natural Science Establishment Addition, Ward Papers, accessed November 28, 2022, https://wardproject.org/items/show/13210.

66. The mummified legs and heads listed in Ward's January 1, 1877, ledger are Peruvian. The wrapped heads of Peruvian mummies were valued at $20 each,

and an entire "Mummy from Chancay" (north of Lima) was listed in 1879 for $65. See Appendix 2, "Henry Ward's Peruvian Mummies."

67. These figures more than double the value of Egyptian material owned by Ward at the time of the 1869 fire, reported as $500 in Inventory A and B (September 3, 1869), Ward Papers.

68. For instance, *Ward's Natural Science Bulletin* 1.2 (1882): 13, under the heading "Skulls of Races" that includes Nubian, Cheyenne, Pawnee, and Sioux heads for sale.

69. Ward, "Contract (Louisville Industrial Exposition)," Ward Papers, accessed November 13, 2022, https://wardproject.org/items/show/16781.

70. "A Biblical Museum," *Ward's Natural Science Bulletin* 1.1 (June 1, 1881): 11. Ward, traveling across the South Pacific at the time, had been notified of the sale in March: Arthur B. Baker letter to Henry Augustus Ward (March 18, 1881).

71. Augustus H. Strong, *Henry A. Ward: Reminiscence and Appreciation* (Rochester, NY: Rochester Historical Society, 1922).

72. "Cornell University," *Ward's Natural Science Bulletin* 2.1 (January 1, 1883): 8.

73. *New York Times*, January 26, 1884; *Chicago Daily Tribune*, January 27, 1884; *Galveston Daily News*, July 27, 1884. See also *Guide to the Campus of Cornell University* (Fulton, NY: Morrill Press, 1920), 25; and https://anthropology.cornell.edu/history-anthropology-collections. None of these mentions Ward's.

74. *Daily Wabash Express*, February 1, 1884.

75. *Cornell Daily Sun*, June 4, 1884; *Chicago Daily Tribune*, June 12, 1884; *Philadelphia Inquirer*, July 22, 1884; *Cheboygan Northern Tribune*, November 6, 1884.

76. So far, no mummy has been found in Ward's correspondence with President White on other matters.

77. Much is now known about Pahat thanks to studies conducted in 2007 by the Berkshire Museum and the Akhmim Mummy Studies Consortium led by Dr. Jonathan Elias. Consult Jonathan Elias, "Shep-en-min: Report of findings from the CT scan of Vassar College CC79.001 With comparative discussion of the mummy of his father Pahat (Berkshire Museum 1903.7.44)," Akhmim Mummy Studies Consortium Research Paper 15-1 (Carlisle, PA: AMSC Research, 2008).

78. Pahat soon drew appreciative crowds to the Berkshire Museum. One second-grader's report after visiting the museum was printed in the local newspaper (*Berkshire Evening Eagle*, June 13, 1914): "There was a mummy in the museum. He was alive in Egypt. When he died Mr. Crane brought it to Pittsfield. The city of Pittsfield papered it, then taped. It was very interesting."

79. Roy Hopping to Zenas Crane, July 9, 1902. I thank Jonathan Elias for sharing copies of this correspondence from the Berkshire Museum.

80. E. Ickes to Roy Hopping, July 7, 1902.

81. Roy Hopping to Zenas Crane, July 9, 1902.

81. Roy Hopping to Zenas Crane, July 9, 1902.
82. E. Ickes to Zenas Crane, March 10, 1903.
83. *New York Daily Tribune,* January 12, 1896, a story picked up also by other newspapers, such as the front page of *Edgefield (South Carolina) Advertiser,* March 11, 1896, from the *Rochester Post-Express.*
84. *Plymouth (Indiana)Semi-Weekly Independent,* March 14, 1896.
85. Ward, *Henry A. Ward,* 201.
86. Not counting whole mummies, the MNI (Minimum Number of Individuals) despoiled by Ward is twenty based on left legs in the Ward's inventories; a maximum number depends on whether right legs, heads, and arms came from other individuals.
87. Hartshorn was forced to renegotiate his debts in a series of letters to Ward (May 28, 1874).
88. Newell Yost Osborne, *A Select School: The History of Mount Union College* (Alliance, OH: Mt. Union College, 1967), 371–375.
89. Osborne, *A Select School,* 374; see also *Wheeling Intelligencer,* September 19, 1873, on the mummy's loan to the Indianapolis Exposition.
90. Osborne, *A Select School,* 375. The date is fixed by a reference to the use of X-rays in a mummy exhibition at the 1939–1940 New York World's Fair. See also "Hand-Made Mummy at Mount Union," *Zanesville (Ohio) Signal,* June 3, 1940, and "Mount Union Now 'Board' with Mummy," *Norwalk Reflector-Herald,* June 3, 1940.
91. *Goshen (New York) Democrat,* May 27, 1874.
92. William Temple Hornaday and William Jacob Holland, *Taxidermy and Zoological Collecting* (New York: Scribner's, 1891), 33.
93. Hornaday and Holland, *Taxidermy and Zoological Collecting,* 100, and Oliver Davie, *Methods in the Art of Taxidermy* (Columbus, OH: Hann and Adair, 1894), 3.
94. *Washington (DC) Evening Star,* July 5, 1906.
95. *Berkshire County Eagle,* October 2, 1907.

Chapter 6

1. Arthur Conan Doyle, *A Study in Scarlet* (1887).
2. One assessment claims: "By the end of the nineteenth century ... the mummy's power as spectacle was confined to the museum." See Nicholas Daly, "That Obscure Object of Desire: Victorian Commodity Culture and Fictions of the Mummy," *Novel: A Forum on Fiction* 28 (1994): 25.
3. HMNS Accession No. 725, item 291 (two-piece coffin) and 292 (human mummy) with the notation: "Acquired by HMNS when Tx. A&M University Museum was disbanded."

4. A tribute to Francis appeared in *Texas A&M Battalion*, October 26, 1927.
5. *Dallas Morning News*, August 24, 1969, and October 22, 1977.
6. Letter of Lutz to Ball, HMNS collection.
7. *Texas A&M Battalion*, February 15, 1940; March 19, 1940; April 30, 1940.
8. Statuettes: *Texas A&M Battalion*, January 11, 1928; tablets: *Texas A&M Battalion*, July 23, 1941.
9. This common goal was lampooned in *Philadelphia Times*, January 27, 1884.
10. Lewis Gould, *Alexander Watkins Terrell* (Austin: University of Texas Press, 2004), 134, 165, and 194. See also *Dallas Morning News*, October 9, 1972.
11. The mummy of Tu Tu, now in the Mabee-Gerrer Museum of Art in Shawnee, Oklahoma. The university closed in 2017. For context, see *Oklahoma City Daily Oklahoman*, January 12, 1958.
12. Jane Beckman, "The Monk, the Mummy and Mabee," *Oklahoma Today* (November–December 1985): 122–127.
13. *Houston Daily Post*, November 10, 1917.
14. *Indianapolis Daily Standard*, January 12, 1885.
15. *Bryan Daily Eagle*, July 10, 1923.
16. *Bryan Daily Eagle*, July 20, 1926.
17. *Bryan Daily Eagle*, May 5, 1927.
18. *Bryan Daily Eagle*, November 27, 1933.
19. *Texas A&M Battalion*, April 1, 1931. In the 1980s when I first visited the A&M archives, there were no known references to the mummy in the available *Battalion* indices, but that has changed dramatically with the subsequent digitization of materials.
20. *Port Arthur News*, September 6, 1929; *Timpson Weekly Times*, September 13, 1929.
21. *Lowell Daily Sun*, August 6, 1894.
22. *Texas A&M Battalion*, December 16, 1938.
23. Jesse Lyman Hurlbut, *The Story Of Chautauqua* (New York: G. P. Putnam's Sons, 1921).
24. *New York Times*, June 15, 1924.
25. *The Chautauquan* 33 (1901): 203.
26. For examples: Otis Mason, "A Group of Mummies," *The Chautauquan* 5 (1884–1885): 572; Frederick Davenport, "A Reading Journey in the Orient," *The Chautauquan* 32 (1900–1901): 178–191.
27. *Wichita (Texas) Daily Times*, November 12, 1912.
28. *Wichita (Texas) Daily Times*, July 5, 1914.
29. *Wichita (Texas) Daily Times*, July 7, 1914, and July 8, 1914.
30. *Wichita (Texas) Daily Times*, July 10, 1914.
31. *Wichita (Texas) Weekly Times*, July 17, 1914.
32. Edwin E. Howell letters to Henry Ward (April 14, 1881, and May 26, 1881); Arthur B. Baker letters to Henry Ward (June 2, 1881, and July 21, 1881).
33. *Ward's Natural Science Bulletin* 1.1 (1881): 11.

34. Alice Stevenson, *Scattered Finds: Archaeology, Egyptology and Museums* (London: UCL Press, 2019), 75.
35. *Texas A&M Battalion*, July 21, 1976. This article claims that Francis received the mummy as a gift.
36. *Texas A&M Battalion*, July 21, 1976.
37. This lab produced the world's only supply of hog cholera serum, the sale of which financed the museum and other operations on campus. On the museum, see *Texas A&M Battalion*, March 19, 1940.
38. The museum's cases were built by a geology student named Huesse: *Texas A&M Battalion*, November 9, 1961.
39. *Dallas Morning News*, June 4, 1939.
40. *Texas A&M Battalion*, September 7, 1943.
41. *Texas A&M Battalion*, August 18, 1944.
42. *Texas A&M Battalion*, January 3, 1947.
43. *Texas A&M Battalion*, July 9, 1948.
44. Before the phrase "funerary offering" the word "royal" has been omitted on the label.
45. *Texas A&M Battalion*, February 8, 1949.
46. *Alice (Texas) Daily Echo*, March 5, 1950; *Texas A&M Battalion*, March 23, 1950.
47. *Texas A&M Battalion*, September 7, 1943; *Dallas Morning News*, October 9, 1972; *Texas A&M Battalion*, November 3, 1977.
48. *Texas A&M Battalion*, November 3, 1977.
49. *Texas A&M Battalion*, December 4, 1980.
50. *Texas A&M Battalion*, December 4, 1980.
51. *Texas A&M Battalion*, June 20, 1951.
52. *Texas A&M Battalion*, November 9, 1961.
53. *Texas A&M Battalion*, March 13, 1963.
54. *Texas A&M Battalion*, March 21, 1963, and March 31, 1963.
55. Evelyn Oppenheimer, ed., *Tolbert of Texas: The Man and his Work* (Fort Worth: Texas Christian University Press, 1986).
56. *Dallas Morning News*, October 24, 1965. The column includes the photo that first appeared in *Dallas Morning News*, June 4, 1939.
57. *Dallas Morning News*, April 28, 1966.
58. He sometimes became confused about the chronology, for example writing in 1969 that he had searched for the mummy about six or seven years earlier, when in fact it was only about four years earlier: *Dallas Morning News*, October 24, 1965, and August 24, 1969. Also, in 1966 Tolbert remembered the mummy as "well preserved" and in 1969 he recalled that it "was dusty but in good shape."
59. *Dallas Morning News*, August 24, 1969.
60. *Dallas Morning News*, October 9, 1972.

61. *Dallas Morning News*, October 9, 1972, and earlier in *Dallas Morning News*, August 24, 1969.
62. *Dallas Morning News*, October 22, 1972.
63. *Dallas Morning News*, October 22, 1977.
64. HMNS Accession records, for which I thank associate registrar Donna Meadows.
65. *Texas A&M Battalion*, November 3, 1977.
66. *Bryan-College Station Eagle*, January 30, 1988.
67. Significantly, the story appeared at the time of the movie release of *Night at the Museum*: https://www.chron.com/life/article/Museum-guard-has-stories-to-rival-Hollywood-1847244.php.
68. Frank Holt, "Egyptomania: Have We Cursed the Pharaohs?," *Archaeology* 39 (March–April 1986): 60–63.
69. *The Mummy Returns* (2001), *The Scorpion King* (2002), and *The Mummy: Tomb of the Dragon Emperor* (2008). See https://www.the-numbers.com/movies/franchise/Mummy#tab=summary.
70. As observed by Heather Pringle, *The Mummy Congress: Science, Obsession, and the Everlasting Dead* (New York: Theia, 2001), 17–19.
71. Pringle, *The Mummy Congress*, 33.

Appendix 2

1. On the lively and illicit trade of Peruvian antiquities in this period, see Christopher Carter, Flora Vilches, and Calogero M. Santoro, "South American Mummy Trafficking," *Journal of the History of Collections* 29 (2017): 395–407.
2. Ward's inventory, listing the legs at three dollars each and the head at twenty. The skull was valued at fifteen dollars.
3. Ward's inventory for January 1, 1879.
4. Letter of Edwin Howell to Henry Ward dated May 22, 1883.
5. *Interpres* (1906): 148.
6. *Croceus* (1917): 221.
7. *Ward's Natural Science Bulletin* 1.2 (1882): 13.

GLOSSARY OF GODS AND TECHNICAL TERMS

Aker An earth deity often taking the form of twin lions that protected the dead.

Akh The resurrected self that passed into the afterlife.

Ammit the Devourer A composite creature (crocodile, lioness, and hippopotamus) that disposed of those found wanting in the final judgment.

Ammon The Greek rendering of the name Amun, generally assimilated as Zeus.

Amun One of the primordial deities of Egypt, associated with the air and later merged with Ra/Re the sun god by the Egyptians (Amun-Ra/Amun-Re) and Zeus by the Greeks (Zeus-Ammon).

Anubis The jackal-headed protector of necropolises who oversaw embalming and the judgment of the dead.

Apis bull A sacred bull, selected for its markings and worshiped in a shrine at Memphis, mummified at death and replaced by another in a continuous cycle.

Atum The procreative sun god who brought into existence the world and whose worship centered upon Heliopolis in lower Egypt.

autolysis The decomposition of a corpse by enzymes escaping from cells within the body.

Ba The active embodiment of a dead person's personality, often depicted as a human-headed bird.

Bes A dwarfish deity associated with childbirth and domestic life in Egypt.

bitumen A dark viscous substance associated with mummification.

canopic jar One of the four vessels used to contain the organs removed during mummification.

cartonnage A material made of papyrus and glue, resembling papier-mâché, that was often painted and placed on a mummy.

computer tomography (CT scan) A medical imaging technique, more advanced than X-rays, now applied to the study of mummies.

dendrochronology The scientific study of tree rings as a precise measure of time.

dragoman A local go-between who served as a guide and interpreter for visitors in the Middle East.

Duamutef A son of Horus, usually represented with a jackal's head and associated with the embalmed stomach.

excerebration The removal of the brain as part of ancient Egyptian mummification.

Frankenmummy A composite mummy formed from the bodies of several individuals.

Hades The Greek god of the underworld and his realm of the dead.

Hapi A son of Horus, usually represented with the head of an ape and associated with the embalmed lungs.

Hathor A maternal goddess depicted as a cow or as a woman wearing a headdress of cow horns and a sun disk.

Horus The falcon-headed son of Osiris and Isis who avenged his father.

Imsety A son of Horus, usually represented with a human head and associated with the embalmed liver.

Isis The sister-wife of Osiris and mother of Horus.

Ka A person's life force, created at birth and eternal, depicted as two upraised arms.

Maat The goddess of justice and cosmic harmony.

mumia vera aegyptiaca A medicinal powder made from pulverized mummies.

mumiyah Arabic word for a kind of bitumen, which has become our term "mummy."

natron A naturally occurring compound mined in Egypt's Wadi Natrun, used as a drying agent during mummification.

Nephthys Sibling of Osiris and Isis, and the sister-wife of Seth.

nomarch A district governor in ancient Egypt.

Nut Winged or star-spangled goddess of the sky and the mother of Osiris, Seth, Isis, and Nephthys.

Osiris God of the dead and underworld whose resurrection rendered him the prototypical mummy.

Ptah A creator god often shown with green skin and a beard.

Ptah-Sokar-Osiris A composite funerary deity representing birth, death, and resurrection.

Qubehsenuef A son of Horus, usually represented with a hawk's head and associated with the embalmed intestines.

Ra or Re God of the sun and sky.

radiocarbon dating A scientific method for estimating the age of organic materials based on the amount of carbon 14 isotope present in a sample.

sah A divine name used in Egypt for the body and its survival as a mummy.

satrap A regional governor within the Persian Empire.

satrapy One of the large regional districts, such as Egypt, that formed the Persian Empire.

scarab A representation of the dung beetle (from Latin singular *scarabeus*, plural *scarabei*), which symbolized the perpetually regenerative sun, used as an amulet.

Schistosoma haematobium A parasite hosted by freshwater snails that afflicts the kidneys, bladder, liver, and spleen.

Serapeum A temple complex at Ṣaqqārah dedicated to Osiris-Apis (Greek *Serapis*) where the mummified Apis bulls were interred.

Seth The murderous, jealous brother of Osiris.

shen **ring** An Egyptian symbol of eternity and regeneration, originally appearing as a rope tied into a loop.

soma heilismenon A Greek phrase meaning "wrapped-up person," used in antiquity as a euphemism for a mummy.

tarichos A Greek word meaning salted meat, used in Egypt as a euphemism for mummy.

Thoth Egyptian god associated with the moon and writing, often depicted with the head of an ibis.

SELECT BIBLIOGRAPHY

Abbott, Henry. *Catalogue of a Collection of Egyptian Antiquities*. New York: Edwin Varey, 1853.

Adams, Judith, and Chrissie Alsop. "Imaging in Egyptian Mummies." In *Egyptian Mummies and Modern Science*. Edited by Rosalie David. Pp. 21–42. Cambridge: Cambridge University Press, 2008.

Allen, Grant. "My New Year's Eve Among the Mummies." *Belgravia Magazine Annual* 37 (1879): 93–105.

Anđelković, Branislav, and Jonathan Elias. "CT Scan of Nesmin from Akhmim: New Data on the Belgrade Mummy." *Issues in Ethnology and Anthropology* 16 (2021): 761–794.

Asirvatham, Sulochana. "The Alexander Romance Tradition from Egypt to Ethiopia." In *Alexander in Africa*. Edited by Philip Bosman. Pp. 109–127. Pretoria: Classical Association of South Africa, 2014.

Aufderheide, Arthur. *The Scientific Study of Mummies*. Cambridge: Cambridge University Press, 2003.

Austin, Jane G. "After Three Thousand Years." *Putnam's Magazine* 2 (July 1868): 38–45.

Aylesworth, Thomas. *Movie Monsters*. Philadelphia: Lippincott, 1975.

Baber, Tessa. "Ancient Corpses as Curiosities: Mummymania in the Age of Early Travel." *Journal of Ancient Egyptian Interconnections* 8 (2016): 60–93.

Baber, Tessa. "Early Travellers and the Animal 'Mummy Pits' of Egypt." In *Creatures of Earth, Water, and Sky*. Edited by Stéphanie Porcier, Salima Ikram, and Stéphane Pasquali. Pp. 67–86. Leiden: Sidestone Press, 2019.

Banes, Steve, ed. *Classic Monsters of Pre-Code Horror Comics: Mummies*. San Diego: IDW Publishing, 2017.

Barrow, Mark, Jr. "The Specimen Dealer: Entrepreneurial Natural History in America's Gilded Age." *Journal of the History of Biology* 33 (Winter 2000): 493–534.

Beckman, Jane. "The Monk, the Mummy and Mabee." *Oklahoma Today* (November–December 1985): 122–127.

Belzoni, Giovanni. *Narrative of the Operations and Recent Discoveries within the Pyramids, Temples, Tombs, and Excavations, in Egypt and Nubia.* London: John Murray, 1820.

Bingen, Jean. *Hellenistic Egypt: Monarchy, Society, Economy, Culture.* Berkeley: University of California Press, 2007.

Black, Andy. *The Dead Walk.* London: Noir, 2000.

Blackwood, Algernon. *John Silence, Physician Extraordinary.* Boston: John W. Luce, 1909.

Blumenbach, John Frederick. "Observations on Some Egyptian Mummies Opened in London." *Philosophical Transactions of the Royal Society of London* 84 (1794): 177–195.

Bodin, Jean. *Colloquium of the Seven about Secrets of the Sublime.* Translated by Marion Kuntz. University Park: Pennsylvania State University, 2008.

Booth, Charlotte. *The Curse of the Mummy.* Oxford: Oneworld, 2009.

Bosworth, A. B. *A Historical Commentary on Arrian's History of Alexander.* Vol. 1, *Commentary on Books I–III.* Oxford: Clarendon Press, 1980.

Brier, Bob. *Egyptomania.* New York: Palgrave Macmillan, 2013.

Brier, Bob. *Tutankhamun and the Tomb That Changed the World.* Oxford: Oxford University Press, 2023.

Brier, Bob, and Daniel Friedman. "Ancient Egypt in the Comics." *KMT* 32 (Fall 2021): 56–67.

Burne-Jones, Georgiana. *Memorials of Edward Burne-Jones.* New York: Macmillan, 1906.

Burstein, Stanley. "Prelude to Alexander: The Reign of Khababash." *Ancient History Bulletin* 14 (2000): 149–154.

Carr, Robert Spencer. "Spider-Bite." *Weird Tales* 7 (June 1926): 735–750 and 863–864.

Carter, Christopher, Flora Vilches, and Calogero M. Santoro. "South American Mummy Trafficking." *Journal of the History of Collections* 29 (2017): 395–407.

Čavka, Mislav, et al. "CT-Guided Endoscopic Recovery of a Foreign Object from the Cranial Cavity of an Ancient Egyptian Mummy." *RSNA RadioGraphics* 32 (2012): 2151–2157.

Cockburn, Aidan, and Eve Cockburn, eds. *Mummies, Diseases, and Ancient Cultures.* Cambridge: Cambridge University Press, 1983.

Cockitt, J. A., S. O. Martin, and R. David. "A New Assessment of the Radiocarbon Age of Manchester Mummy No. 1770." *Yearbook of Mummy Studies* 2 (2014): 95–102.

Cook, Paul. *Grafton Elliot Smith, Egyptology and the Diffusion of Culture.* Brighton: Sussex Academic Press, 2012.

Cosmacini, Paola, and Patrizia Piacentini. "Notes on the History of the Radiological Study of Egyptian Mummies: From X-Rays to New Imaging Techniques." *La Radiologia Medica* 113 (2008): 615–626.

Daly, Nicholas. "That Obscure Object of Desire: Victorian Commodity Culture and Fictions of the Mummy." *Novel: A Forum on Fiction* 28 (1994): 24–51.

Dannenfeldt, Karl. "Egyptian Mumia: The Sixteenth Century Experience and Debate." *Sixteenth Century Journal* 16 (1985): 163–180.

d'Athanasi, Giovanni. *A Brief Account of the Researches and Discoveries in Upper Egypt.* London: John Hearne, 1836.

Davenport, Frederick. "A Reading Journey in the Orient." *The Chautauquan* 32 (1900–1901): 178–191.

Davey, Marie Janet, Pamela Craig, and Olaf Heino Drummer. "Dislodged Teeth in Four Intact Child Mummies from Graeco-Roman Egypt (332 BCE–c. 395 CE)." *Papers on Anthropology* 23 (2014): 18–28.

David, Rosalie. *Handbook to Life in Ancient Egypt.* Oxford: Oxford University Press, 1998.

David, Rosalie. "Medical Science and Egyptology." In *Egyptology Today.* Edited by Richard Wilkinson. Pp. 36–54. Cambridge: Cambridge University Press, 2008.

David, Rosalie. *A Year in the Life of Ancient Egypt.* Barnsley: Pen and Sword, 2015.

David, Rosalie, ed. *Manchester Museum Mummy Project.* Manchester: Manchester University Press, 1979.

David, Rosalie, and Rick Archbold. *Conversations with Mummies.* New York: William Morrow, 2000.

David, Rosalie, and Eileen Murphy, eds. *The Life and Times of Takabuti in Ancient Egypt: Investigating the Belfast Mummy.* Liverpool: Liverpool University Press, 2021.

Davidson, John. *An Address on Embalming Generally, Delivered at the Royal Institution on the Unrolling of a Mummy.* London: James Ridgway, 1833.

Davie, Oliver. *Methods in the Art of Taxidermy.* Columbus: Hann and Adair, 1894.

Dawson, Warren R. "Pettigrew's Demonstrations upon Mummies. A Chapter in the History of Egyptology." *Journal of Egyptian Archaeology* 20 (1934): 170–182.

Dawson, Warren R., and P. H. K. Gray. *Catalogue of the Egyptian Antiquities in the British Museum.* Vol. 1, *Mummies and Human Remains.* London: British Museum, 1969.

Day, Jasmine. *The Mummy's Curse: Mummymania in the English-Speaking World.* London: Routledge, 2006.

Day, Jasmine. "'Thinking Makes It So': Reflections on the Ethics of Displaying Egyptian Mummies." *Papers on Anthropology* 23 (2014): 29–44.

della Valle, Pietro. *Voyages de Pietro Della Valle, gentilhomme romain.* Vol. 1. St. Martin-sur-Renelle: Robert Machuel, 1745.

Dennett, Andrea. *Weird and Wonderful: The Dime Museum in America*. New York: New York University Press, 1997.

Disbrow, Jay. "The Mummy's Hand." *Ghostly Weird Stories* 120 (September 1953): 1–9.

Douglas, James. *Two Mummies from Thebes, in Upper Egypt*. Quebec: Huner, Rose and Co., 1865.

Doyle, Arthur Conan. "Lot No. 249." *Harper's Magazine* (September 1892): 525–544.

Doyle, Arthur Conan. "The Ring of Thoth." *Cornhill Magazine* (January 1890): 46–61.

Dunand, Françoise, and Roger Lichtenberg. *Mummies and Death in Egypt*. Ithaca, NY: Cornell University Press, 2006.

Dunn, John B. *Perilous Trails of Texas*. Dallas: Southwest Press, 1932.

Dupras, Tosha, Sandra M. Wheeler, Lana Williams, and Peter Sheldrick. "Birth in Ancient Egypt: Timing, Trauma, and Triumph?" In *Egyptian Bioarchaeology: Humans, Animals, and the Environment*. Edited by Salima Ikram, J. Kaiser, and R. Walker. Pp. 53–65. Leiden: Sidestone Press, 2015.

Durel, John. "In Pursuit of a Profit." In *Mermaids, Mummies, and Mastodons: The Emergence of the American Museum*. Edited by William Alderson. Pp. 41–47. Washington, DC: American Association of Museums, 1992.

Edwards, Amelia. "Lying in State in Cairo." *Harper's New Monthly Magazine* 65 (1882): 200.

Edwards, Amelia. *A Thousand Miles Up the Nile*. 2nd ed. London: Routledge, 1890; reprint 2008.

Elias, Jonathan. "General Analysis of the Mummy of Padihershef at Massachusetts General Hospital." Akhmim Mummy Studies Consortium Research Paper 14-1. Carlisle, PA: AMSC Research, 2014.

Elias, Jonathan. "Overview of Lininger A06696, a Mummy and Coffin at the University of Nebraska, Lincoln." Akhmim Mummy Studies Consortium Research Paper 16-2. Carlisle, PA: AMSC Research, 2016.

Elias, Jonathan. "Overview of UNL 15-10-97, an Akhmimic Mummy and Coffin at the University of Nebraska, Lincoln (Rominger's Mummy)." Akhmim Mummy Studies Consortium Research Paper 16-4. Carlisle, PA: AMSC Research, 2016.

Elias, Jonathan. "Shep-en-min: Report of Findings from the CT Scan of Vassar College CC79.001 with Comparative Discussion of the Mummy of His Father Pahat (Berkshire Museum 1903.7.44)." Akhmim Mummy Studies Consortium Research Paper 15-1. Carlisle, PA: AMSC Research, 2008.

Elliott, Chris. "Bandages, Bitumen, Bodies and Business—Egyptian Mummies as Raw Materials." *Aegyptiaca Journal of the History of Reception of Ancient Egypt* 1 (2017): 26–46.

Everson, William. *Classics of the Horror Film*. Secaucus, NJ: Citadel, 1974.

Fairchild, Herman L. "Ward's Natural Science Establishment." *Scientific Monthly* 26 (May 1928): 468–471.

Farman, Elbert. *Along the Nile with General Grant.* New York: Grafton Press, 1904.

Fletcher, Alexandra, Daniel Antoine, and J. D. Hill, eds. *Regarding the Dead: Human Remains in the British Museum.* London: British Museum, 2014.

Forbes, Dennis. "Everybody Loves a Parade." *KMT* 32 (2021): 12–13.

Forbes, Dennis, Salima Ikram, and Janice Kamrin. "Tutankhamen's Missing Ribs." *KMT* 18 (2007): 50–56.

Fritze, Ronald. *Egyptomania: A History of Fascination, Obsession and Fantasy.* London: Reaktion Books, 2016.

Frost, Brian. *The Essential Guide to Mummy Literature.* Lanham, MD: Scarecrow Press, 2008.

Gautier, Théophile. *The Romance of a Mummy.* New York: J. Bradburn, 1863.

Germer, Renate. "Problems of Science in Egyptology." In *Science in Egyptology.* Edited by Rosalie David. Pp. 521–525. Manchester: Manchester University Press, 1986.

Gessler-Löhr, Beatrix. "Mummies and Mummification." In *The Oxford Handbook of Roman Egypt.* Edited by Christina Riggs. Pp. 664–683. Oxford: Oxford University Press, 2012.

Gifford, William, ed. *The Dramatic Works and Poems of James Shirley.* Vol. 2. London: John Murray, 1833.

Gill-Robinson, Heather, Jonathan Elias, Frank Bender, Travis T. Allard, and Robert D. Hoppa. "Using Image Analysis Software to Create a Physical Skull Model for the Facial Reconstruction of a Wrapped Akhmimic Mummy." *Journal of Computing and Information Technology* 14 (2006): 45–51.

Glut, Donald. *Classic Movie Monsters.* London: Scarecrow, 1978.

Glynn, Basil. *The Mummy on Screen: Orientalism and Monstrosity in Horror Cinema.* London: Bloomsbury Academic, 2020.

Gould, Lewis. *Alexander Watkins Terrell.* Austin: University of Texas Press, 2004.

Graf, Otto Theodor. *Catalogue of the Theodor Graf Collection of Unique Ancient Greek Portraits 2000 Years Old Recently Discovered and Now on View in Old Vienna, Midway Plaisance at the World's Columbian Exposition, Chicago.* Privately printed.

Gray, P. H. K. "Embalmers' 'Restorations.'" *Journal of Egyptian Archaeology* 52 (1966): 138–140.

Gray, P. H. K. "Radiography of Ancient Egyptian Mummies." *Medical Radiography and Photography* 43 (1967): 34–44.

Greco, Mark, et al. "X-Ray Computerized Tomography as a New Method in Monitoring *Amegilla holmsi* Nest Structures, Nesting Behavior, and Adult Female Activity." *Entomologia Experimentalis et Applicata* 120 (2006): 71–76.

Griffith, George. "The Lost Elixir." *Pall Mall Magazine* 31 (1903): 154–165.

Haggard, Henry Rider. *She: A History of Adventure.* New York: Harpers, 1886.

Halliwell, Leslie. *The Dead That Walk.* London: Grafton, 1986.

Harrell, James, and Michael Lewan. "Sources of Mummy Bitumen in Ancient Egypt and Palestine." *Archaeometry* 44 (2002): 285–293.

Harris, James, and Kent Weeks. *X-Raying the Pharaohs*. New York: Charles Scribner's Sons, 1973.

Hawass, Zahi, and Sahar Saleem. *Scanning the Pharaohs*. Cairo: American University in Cairo Press, 2016.

Hernández, Raquel Martín. "Faience Mummy Labels Written in Greek." *Zeitschrift für Papyrologie und Epigraphik* 208 (2018): 193–202.

Heron, E., and H. Heron. "The Story of Baelbrow." *Pearson's Magazine* 5 (April 1898): 366–375.

Hertzog, Christian. *Essay de mumio-graphie*. Gotha: Jean Reyher, 1718.

Holt, Frank. *Alexander the Great and the Mystery of the Elephant Medallions*. Berkeley: University of California Press, 2003.

Holt, Frank. "Egyptomania: Have We Cursed the Pharaohs?" *Archaeology* (March–April 1986): 60–63.

Holt, Frank. "I, Eternal Bodyguard." *Aramco World* 71 (March–April 2020): 32–37.

Holt, Frank. "I, Horn of Africa." *Aramco World* 69 (January–February 2018): 26–31.

Holt, Frank. "Mystery Mummy: Unraveling the Remains of Ankh-Hap the Egyptian." *Archaeology* (November–December 1991): 44–51.

Holt, Frank. *The Treasures of Alexander the Great*. Oxford: Oxford University Press, 2016.

Hornaday, William Temple. "The King of Museum Builders." *Commercial Travelers' Home Magazine* 6 (February 1896): 147–159.

Hornaday, William Temple. *Two Years in the Jungle: The Experiences of a Hunter and Naturalist in India, Ceylon, the Malay Peninsula and Borneo*. London: Kegan Paul, Trench, 1885.

Hornaday, William Temple, and William Jacob Holland. *Taxidermy and Zoological Collecting*. New York: Scribner's, 1891.

Hunt, Arthur, and Campbell Edgar. *Select Papyri*. Vol. 1. Cambridge, MA: Harvard University Press, 1988.

Hurlbut, Jesse Lyman. *The Story of Chautauqua*. New York: G. P. Putnam's Sons, 1921.

Ikram, Salima. *Death and Burial in Ancient Egypt*. London: Longman, 2003.

Ikram, Salima, and Aidan Dodson. *The Mummy in Ancient Egypt: Equipping the Dead for Eternity*. London: Thames and Hudson, 1998.

Irish, John, ed. *A Mummy Omnibus: 1820s–1920s*. Bridgeport, TX: A Bit O'Irish Press, 2018.

Jimenez, Lissette. "From Birth to Rebirth: Perceptions of Childhood in Greco-Roman Egypt." In *Childhood in Antiquity*. Edited by Lesley Beaumont, Matthew Dillon, and Nicola Harrington. Pp. 121–133. New York: Routledge, 2021.

Jones, Nigel. *Rupert Brooke: Life, Death and Myth*. London: Richard Cohen, 1999.

Kalampoukas, Kiriakos, et al. "Crafting a Corpse, 'Cheating' the Gods: A Composite Mummy from Ancient Egypt Studied with Computed Tomography." *International Journal of Osteoarchaeology* 30 (2020): 114–118.

Kane, Robert J. "James Crossley, Sir Thomas Browne, and the Fragment on Mummies." *Review of English Studies* 9 (1933): 266–274.

Keating, Rex. *The Trumpets of Tutankhamun: Adventures of a Radio Pioneer in the Middle East.* Basingstoke: Fisher Miller, 1999.

Kohlstedt, Sally Gregory. "Henry A. Ward: The Merchant Naturalist and American Museum Development." *Journal of the Society for the Bibliography of Natural History* 9 (1980): 647–661.

Küffer, Alexandra. "Tracing the History of a Coffin and Its Mummy: The Burial Equipment from Gamhud at the Museum of Ethnology in Burgdorf (Switzerland)." In *Ancient Egyptian Coffins: Craft Traditions and Functionality.* Edited by John Taylor and Marie Vandenbeusch. Pp. 415–433. Leuven: Peeters, 2018.

Lacovara, Peter, and Sue D'Auria, eds. *The Mystery of the Albany Mummies.* Albany: Excelsior Editions, 2018.

Ladynin, Ivan. "Overseer of the Wab-Priests of Sekhmet Somtutefnakht: 'Collaborationist' or the Victim of Deportation?" *Vostok* 1 (2014): 18–28 (in Russian).

Legh, Thomas. *Narrative of a Journey in Egypt and the Country beyond the Cataracts.* London: John Murray, 1816.

Lemery, Nicolas. *Traité universel des drogues simples.* 4th ed. Paris: Laurent d'Houry, 1732.

Loreille, Odile, et al. "Biological Sexing of a 4000-Year-Old Egyptian Mummy Head to Assess the Potential of Nuclear DNA Recovery from the Most Damaged and Limited Forensic Specimens." *Genes* 9.3 (2018): 135. https://doi.org/10.3390/genes9030135. PMID: 29494531; PMCID: PMC5867856.

Lovecraft, H. P., and Harry Houdini. "Imprisoned with the Pharaohs." *Weird Tales* 4 (May–July 1924): 3–12.

Luckhurst, Roger. *The Mummy's Curse.* Oxford: Oxford University Press, 2012.

Lushington, Charles. *Narrative of a Journey from Calcutta to Europe, by Way of Egypt in the Years 1827 and 1828.* London: John Murray, 1829.

MacDonald, Sally, and Michael Rice, eds. *Consuming Ancient Egypt.* New York: Routledge, 2009.

Mackay, Charles. *The Twin Soul: The Strange Experiences of Dr. Rameses.* 2 vols. London: Ward and Downey, 1887.

Mansford, Charles. "At the Pyramid of the Sacred Bulls." *Windsor Magazine* 3 (1896): 386–391.

Manuelian, Peter Der. *Walking among Pharaohs: George Reisner and the Dawn of Modern Egyptology.* Oxford: Oxford University Press, 2023.

Marchant, Jo. *The Shadow King: The Bizarre Afterlife of King Tut's Mummy*. Boston: Da Capo Press, 2013.

Markham, Gervase. *The Husbandman's Jewel*. London: G. Conyers, 1695.

Marković, Nenad. "The Cult of the Sacred Bull Apis: History of Study." In *A History of Research into Ancient Egyptian Culture Conducted in Southeast Europe*. Edited by Mladen Tomorad. Pp. 135–144. Oxford: Archaeopress, 2015.

Marković, Nenad. "A Look through His Window: The Sanctuary of the Divine Apis Bull at Memphis." *Journal of Ancient Egyptian Architecture* 1 (2016): 57–70.

Mason, Otis. "A Group of Mummies." *The Chautauquan* 5 (1884–1885): 572.

McClellan, Andrew. "P. T. Barnum, Jumbo the Elephant, and the Barnum Museum of Natural History at Tufts University." *Journal of the History of Collections* 24 (2012): 45–62.

McGeough, Kevin. "Heroes, Mummies, and Treasure: Near Eastern Archaeology in the Movies." *Near Eastern Archaeology* 69 (2006): 174–185.

Moodie, Roy. *Roentgenologic Studies of Egyptian and Peruvian Mummies*. Chicago: Field Museum Press, 1931.

Morton, Samuel George. *Crania Aegyptiaca*. Philadelphia: John Penington, 1844.

Nash, Stephen, and Gary Feinman, eds. *Curators, Collections, and Contexts: Anthropology at the Field Museum, 1893–2002*. Chicago: Field Museum, 2003.

Nelson, Mark. "The Mummy's Curse: Historical Cohort Study." *BMJ* 325 (2002): 1482.

Newkirk, Pamela. *Spectacle: The Astonishing Life of Ota Benga*. New York: Amistad, 2015.

Nielsen, Nicky. *Egyptomaniacs: How We Became Obsessed with Ancient Egypt*. Philadelphia: Pen & Sword, 2020.

O'Brien, J. J., et al. "CT Imaging of Human Mummies: A Critical Review of the Literature (1979–2005)." *International Journal of Osteoarchaeology* 19 (2009): 90–98.

Osborne, Newell Yost. *A Select School: The History of Mount Union College*. Alliance, OH: Mt. Union College, 1967.

Pahl, W. M. "Possibilities, Limitations and Prospects of Computed Tomography as a Non-invasive Method of Mummy Studies." In *Science in Egyptology*. Edited by Rosalie David. Pp. 13–24. Manchester: Manchester University Press, 1986.

Paré, Ambroise. *Discours d'Ambroise Paré, conseiller premier chirurgien du roy, à scavoir, de la mumie, des venins, de la licorne et de la peste*. Paris: Gabriel Buon, 1582.

Peet, T. Eric. *The Great Tomb-Robberies of the Twentieth Egyptian Dynasty*. 2 vols. Oxford: Clarendon Press, 1930.

Pemberton, Clive. *The Weird o'It*. London: Henry Drane, 1906.

Perdu, Olivier. "Le monument de Samtoutefnakht à Naples." *Revue d'Égyptologie* 36 (1985): 99–113.

Pettigrew, Thomas. *A History of Egyptian Mummies*. London: Longman, 1834.

Poe, Edgar Allen. "Some Words with a Mummy." *American Review* 1 (1845): 363–370.

Pringle, Heather. *The Mummy Congress: Science, Obsession, and the Everlasting Dead.* New York: Theia, 2001.

Quinn, Seabury. "The Bleeding Mummy." *Weird Tales* 20 (November 1932): 625–644.

Quinn, Seabury. "The Grinning Mummy." *Weird Tales* 8 (December 1926): 739–754.

Radford, Benjamin. "Bailing in the Mummies." *Skeptical Inquirer* 43 (March–April 2019): 43.

Rae, William Fraser. *Egypt To-day: The First to the Third Khedive.* London: R. Bentley and Son, 1892.

Reid, Howard. *In Search of the Immortals: Mummies, Death and the Afterlife.* London: Headline, 1999.

Reiling, Henri, and Tat'jána Spunarová. "Václav Fricˇ (1839–1916) and His Influence on Collecting Natural History." *Journal of the History of Collections* 17 (2005): 23–43.

Reimer, Paula J., et al. "The IntCal20 Northern Hemisphere Radiocarbon Age Calibration Curve (0–55 cal kBP)." *Radiocarbon* 62 (2020): 725–757.

Renschler, Emily S., and Janet Monge. "The Samuel George Morton Cranial Collection." *Expedition Magazine* 50 (2008): 30–38.

Rice, Anne. *The Mummy or Ramses the Damned.* New York: Ballantine, 1989.

Riggs, Christina. "Ancient Egypt in the Museum: Concepts and Constructions." In *A Companion to Ancient Egypt,* vol. 2. Edited by Alan B. Lloyd. Pp. 1129–1153. Malden, MA: Blackwell, 2010.

Riggs, Christina. *Treasured: How Tutankhamun Shaped a Century.* New York: Public Affairs, 2021.

Riggs, Christina. *Unwrapping Ancient Egypt.* London: Bloomsbury, 2014.

Rohde, Eleanour Sinclair. *The Old English Herbals.* London: Longmans, Green, 1922.

Rohmer, Sax (Arthur Ward). *The Dream Detective.* London: Jarrolds, 1920.

Romer, Isabella. *A Pilgrimage to the Temples and Tombs of Egypt, Nubia, and Palestine in 1845–6.* Vol. 1. London: Richard Bentley, 1846.

Ruffer, Sir Marc. "Note on the Presence of 'Bilharzia haematobia' in Egyptian Mummies of the Twentieth Dynasty [1250–1000 BC]." *British Medical Journal* 1 (1910): 16.

Rühli, Frank J. "Magnetic Resonance Imaging of Ancient Mummies." *Anatomical Record* 298 (2015): 1111–1115.

Savage, Richard. *The Poetical Works of Richard Savage.* Vol. 1. Edinburg: Martine, 1780.

Schiødt, Sofie. *Medical Science in Ancient Egypt: A Translation and Interpretation of Papyrus Louvre-Carlsberg (pLouvre E 32847 + pCarlsberg 917).* Det Humanistiske Fakultet, Københavns Universitet, 2021.

Scholz-Böttcher, Barbara M., Arie Nissenbaum, and Jürgen Rullkötter. "An 18th Century Medication 'Mumia vera aegyptica'—Fake or Authentic?" *Organic Geochemistry* 65 (December 2013): 1–18.

Schwyzer, Philip. "Mummy Is Become Merchandise: Literature and the Anglo-Egyptian Mummy Trade in the Seventeenth Century." In *Re-orienting the Renaissance: Cultural Exchanges with the East.* Edited by Gerald MacLean. Pp. 66–87. London: Palgrave Macmillan, 2005.

Sheppard, Kathleen. "Between Spectacle and Science: Margaret Murray and the Tomb of the Two Brothers." *Science in Context* 25 (2012): 525–549.

Shillaber, Benjamin. *Rhymes with Reason and Without.* Boston: Tompkins and Mussey, 1853.

Shirk, Adam. "Osiris: The Weird Tale of an Egyptian Mummy." *Weird Tales* 1 (June 1923): 55–56.

Slayman, Andrew. "Corpse in the Curiosity Shop." In *Secrets of Ancient Egypt.* Edited by Peter Young et al. P. 25. New York: Hatherleigh Press, 2004.

Smith, Albert. "Mr. Grubbe's Night with Memnon." *Illuminated Magazine* 1 (1845): 31–35.

Smith, Clark Ashton. *Ebony and Crystal: Poems in Verse and Prose.* Auburn, CA: Auburn Journal, 1922.

Smith, Grafton Elliot. *Catalogue général des antiquités égyptiennes du Musée du Caire N° 61051–61100: The Royal Mummies.* Cairo: Institut français d'archéologie orientale, 1912.

Smith, Mark. *Traversing Eternity: Texts for the Afterlife from Ptolemaic and Roman Egypt.* Oxford: Oxford University Press, 2009.

Smith, Stuart. "Unwrapping The Mummy: Hollywood Fantasies, Egyptian Realities." In *Box Office Archaeology: Refining Hollywood's Portrayals of the Past.* Edited by Julie M. Schablitsky. Pp. 16–33. Walnut Creek, CA: Left Coast Press, 2007.

Sowada, Karin, et al. "Who's That Lying in My Coffin? An Imposter Exposed by 14C Dating." *Radiocarbon* 53 (2011): 221–228.

Stephens, John, ed. *Into the Mummy's Tomb.* New York: Barnes and Noble, 2006.

Sterrett, Douglas. "A New Type of Calcite from the Joplin Mining District." *American Journal of Science* 18 (1904): 73–76.

Stevenson, Alice. *Scattered Finds: Archaeology, Egyptology and Museums.* London: UCL Press, 2019.

Stienne, Angela. *Mummified: The Stories behind Egyptian Mummies in Museums.* Manchester: Manchester University Press, 2022.

Stoker, Bram. *The Jewel of Seven Stars.* London: William Heinemann, 1903; rev. ed. London: William Rider & Son, 1912.

Strathern, Paul. *Napoleon in Egypt.* New York: Bantam, 2007.

Straton, Colonel. "Account of the Sepulchral Caverns of Egypt." *Boston Journal of Philosophy and the Arts* 1 (1823): 48–53.

Strong, Augustus H. Henry A. *Ward: Reminiscence and Appreciation*. Rochester, NY: Rochester Historical Society, 1922.

Stuart, Henry Windsor Villiers. *Nile Gleanings Concerning the Ethnology, History and Art of Ancient Egypt*. London: John Murray, 1879.

Sugg, Richard. *Mummies, Cannibals and Vampires: The History of Corpse Medicine from the Renaissance to the Victorians*. 2nd ed. New York: Routledge, 2016.

Sutherland, John. *Jumbo: The Unauthorized Biography of a Victorian Sensation*. London: Aurum Press, 2014.

Taylor, John. "The Collection of Egyptian Mummies in the British Museum: Overview and Potential for Study." In *Regarding the Dead: Human Remains in the British Museum*. Edited by Alexandra Fletcher, Daniel Antoine, and J. D. Hill. Pp. 103–114. London: British Museum, 2014.

Taylor, John. *Egyptian Mummies*. London: British Museum Press, 2010.

Teeter, Emily. "Egypt in Chicago: A Story of Three Collections." In *Millions of Jubilees: Studies in Honor of David P. Silverman*. Vol. 2. Edited by Zahi Hawass and Jennifer Houser Wegner. Pp. 303–314. Cairo: Conseil Suprême des Antiquités de l'Egypte, 2010.

Thompson, Dorothy J. *Memphis under the Ptolemies*. 2nd ed. Princeton, NJ: Princeton University Press, 2012.

Thompson, Jason. *Wonderful Things: A History of Egyptology*. Vol. 1, *From Antiquity to 1881*. Cairo: American University in Cairo Press, 2015.

Töpfer, Susanne. "Theory and Practice / Text and Mummies: The Instructions of the 'Embalming Ritual' in the Light of Archaeological Evidence." In *Burial and Mortuary Practices in Late Period and Graeco-Roman Egypt, Proceedings of the International Conference Held at Museum of Fine Arts, Budapest, 17–19 July 2014*. Edited by Katalin Kóthay. Pp. 23–34. Budapest: Museum of Fine Arts, 2017.

Trafton, Scott. *Egypt Land: Race and Nineteenth-Century American Egyptomania*. Durham, NC: Duke University Press, 2004.

Tyldesley, Joyce. *Tutankhamen's Curse*. London: Profile Books, 2012.

Vance, Robert. "Memorial of George Letchworth English." *American Mineralogist* 30 (1945): 130–134.

Vandenberg, Philipp. *The Curse of the Pharaohs*. New York: Pocket Book, 1977.

Van Siclen, Charles, III. "The Mummy and Coffin of Ankh-hap at the Houston Museum of Natural Science." *Varia Aegyptiaca* 7 (1991): 69–79.

Vasilyev, S. V., et al. "Anthropological Study of the Ancient Egyptian Mummy Based on the Computed Tomography Method." *Anthropology* 6 (2018): 1–6.

Vernus, Pascal. *Affairs and Scandals in Ancient Egypt*. Ithaca, NY: Cornell University Press, 2003.

Vos, R. L. *The Apis Embalming Ritual: P. Vindob. 3873*. Leuven: Peeters, 1993.

Wakeling, T. G. *Forged Egyptian Antiquities*. London: Adam & Charles Black, 1912.

Waldron, H. A. "The Study of the Human Remains from Nubia: The Contribution of Grafton Elliot Smith and His Colleagues to Palaeopathology." *Medical History* 44 (2000): 363–388.

Warren, John C. "Description of an Egyptian Mummy Presented to the Massachusetts General Hospital." *Boston Journal of Philosophy and the Arts* 1 (1823): 164–179 and 269–287.

Webb, Jane. *The Mummy! A Tale of the Twenty-Second Century*. Vol. 1. London: Henry Colburn, 1827.

Wilkinson, John Gardner. *A Handbook for Travelers in Egypt*. 5th ed. London: John Murray, 1876.

Wisseman, Sarah, and David Hunt. "Rescanned: New Results from a Child Mummy at the University of Illinois." *Yearbook of Mummy Studies* 2 (2014): 87–94.

Wolfe, Sue J. "Long under Wraps, Cataloguing Puzzle Solved." *The Book* 61 (November 2003): 4–5.

Wolfe, Sue J. *Mummies in Nineteenth Century America*. London: McFarland, 2009.

Wolohojian, Albert, ed. *The Romance of Alexander the Great by Pseudo-Callisthenes*. New York: Columbia University Press, 1969.

Zimmer, T. *Les Grottes des crocodiles de Maabdah*. San Antonio, TX: Van Siclen, 1987.

Zytaruk, Maria. "American's First Circulating Museum: The Object Collection of the Library Company of Philadelphia." *Museums History Journal* 10 (2017): 68–82.

INDEX

For the benefit of digital users, indexed terms that span two pages (e.g., 52–53) may, on occasion, appear on only one of those pages.

Tables are indicated by *t* following the page number